SOUL
MATTERS

FOR TEENS

Wisdom & Inspiration
for the Most Important
Issues of Your Life

Published by J. Countryman® a division of Thomas Nelson, Inc., Nashville, Tennessee 37214

Managing editor: Jessica Inman

For a list of acknowledgements, see page 254-255.

Unless otherwise indicated, Scripture quotations are taken from *The Holy Bible*,
New Century Version, copyright © 1987, 1988, 1991 by Word Publishing,
Dallas, Texas 75039. Used by permission.

Scriptures marked NKJV are taken from The New King James Version.
Copyright © 1979, 1980, 1982, Thomas Nelson, Inc.

Scripture quotations marked CEV are taken from the Contemporary English Version,
copyright © 1991, 1992, 1995 by the American Bible Society. Used by permission.

www.jcountryman.com
www.thomasnelson.com

Designed by Jackson Design Company LLC, Springdale, Arkansas

ISBN #1404102035

Printed in China

SOUL
MATTERS

FOR TEENS

A Division of Thomas Nelson Publishers
Since 1798

www.thomasnelson.com

Contents

Take Care of Your Soul

What good is it if someone gains the whole world—but loses their soul?

In our mad-dash, non-stop way of life, we too often forget about—or blatantly ignore—what matters most for our lives. But deep down, the simple truth that nothing—no achievements, no pleasures, no possessions—equals the value of the human soul, resonates in our inner being. Because what we most want for ourselves is to live our lives with significance and meaning. We long to be all that God created us to be.

If you have found yourself too busy and too distracted by the hundreds of things that clamor for your attention to seek nourishment for your soul; if you have been simply going through the motions of fulfilling God's best plans for your life; if you are ready to stop floating with the currents of a joyless and shallow society in order to see a remarkable difference in your life—and profoundly impact the lives of those around you—then *Soul Matters for Teens* is for you.

Soul Matters for Teens tackles almost fifty of the crucial life issues teens face, weaving together poignant personal reflection questions, inspirational quotes, real life stories from others, God's promises, brief—but hard-hitting—Bible studies, practical life application ideas, and prayer starters to help you to discover for yourself how to let your soul take flight and soar!

When you take care of your soul, your entire life takes flight and soars.
ANONYMOUS

User's Guide

SOUL MATTERS FOR TEENS *is easy to follow and use, but to maximize the benefit you get from this resource, here are a few quick ideas and suggestions for your consideration.*

TO THINK ABOUT

In any area of study, when we understand how a topic relates to our specific circumstances, we experience increased levels of interest, comprehension, and retention. When you ask yourself the questions with each topic, take your time and reflect on recent events in your own life.

LESSON FOR LIFE

These quick, hard-hitting, to-the-point Bible studies are not designed to provide you with everything you need to know and "all the answers" on each of the topics, but they are designed to stimulate your own thinking and discovery learning. You will enhance what is provided here when you take the extra time to look up all the Bible passages that are referenced.

"God Will" Promises

One of the ways our souls take flight is when we truly believe in our hearts that God is good and faithful. These life-changing promises have been embraced and experienced by people of faith for centuries and have stood the test of time. When one of the promises is particularly relevant to your life, take a few extra minutes to memorize the verse so it will always be close to your heart.

REAL LIFE

True life stories are an inspiring way to see how God is at work in the life of others. Some of these stories will be exactly what you need to make some important life changes and decisions. But you don't have to relate to every single person's story to discover dynamics that will help you experience God's presence more fully in your life.

ACTION

Not every Action Step found in *Soul Matters for Teens* will be just right for you. But don't be afraid to stretch yourself and try something you would not normally think of on your own. Or let the ideas found with each soul matter prompt you to come up with an even better way to put truth into practice.

PRAYER

Let this brief prayer starter help you express your own requests, thanksgiving, and praise to God.

TOUGH TIMES

EVEN WHEN LIFE IS TOUGH, YOU CAN TRUST GOD TO HELP YOU SURVIVE AND THRIVE.

When you have nothing left but God, then for the first time you become aware that God is enough.

MAUDE ROYDEN

TO THINK ABOUT

- Have you ever experienced a real tough time when it was tough to trust God?
- What would you say to a friend who feels like their life is helpless?
- How have you seen God help you during difficult times?

LESSON FOR LIFE

PROMISES

God will...

Always love you
Lamentations 3:22

Give you peace
Isaiah 26:3

Be available to help 24/7
Psalm 46:1

Take care of you
Nahum 1:7

When the Going Gets Tough

BIBLE STUDY PASSAGE: 2 CORINTHIANS 12:7-10

God is our protection and our strength. He always helps in times of trouble.

PSALM 46:1

One of the greatest heroes of faith is the Apostle Paul. Churches, hospitals, schools, and even cities are named after him to honor his great contributions to the Church of Jesus Christ. He wrote thirteen letters in the New Testament, and almost half of the book of Acts (chapters 9 and 13-28) is written about his life.

You would think that a man who was that powerful probably had everything go his way. But that is not the case. He had an incredibly tough life. In fact, one Roman historian described him as a short, red-headed, ugly man (Josephus).

Some of the really bad things that happened to him were—

- *He was shipwrecked (Acts 27:13-28:10).*
- *He was attacked by a mob who didn't like his teaching and left for dead (Acts 21:30-32).*

12

- *He was imprisoned for being a Christian (Acts 16:23).*
- *He was criticized by church people who liked other leaders better (2 Corinthians 10:10, 12:11).*
- *He even had physical problems (Galatians 4:13).*

Despite all these incredible difficulties, Paul was joyful (Philippians 2:29)—and he trusted God to take care of him and make him a conqueror (Philippians 4:13).

When life is tough, our souls get discouraged. Don't give up and lose faith. You can trust God!

Don't be afraid, because I have saved you. I have called you by name, and you are mine. When you pass through the waters, I will be with you. When you cross rivers, you will not drown. When you walk through fire, you will not be burned, nor will the flames hurt you.
Isaiah 43:1-2

REAL LIFE

Still Skiing

KENT PALMER AS TOLD TO GLENDA PALMER

After I graduated from high school in southern California, my parents let me fulfill my dream of moving to Lake Tahoe to work at a ski resort during the winter. Later I fulfilled another dream—a helicopter ski trip with my cousin Todd to Banff, British Columbia. When the pilot dropped us off at the top of the mountain, we skied down the pristine slopes uncluttered by other skiers and chair lifts. As I carved turns in the powdery snow, I felt a new closeness to God.

But after that trip, my back began to hurt. I usually didn't worry about sore muscles or aching bones because little injuries here and there were common to me, something to shrug off. I worked in construction and stayed active in sports. But this pain was different. I finally told my mom, "My back hurts so bad I can't surf," so she called for a doctor's appointment. Even Mom wasn't particularly concerned. She said, "You probably pulled something on that ski trip, jumping out of a helicopter, for heaven's sake."

The doctor performed some tests, then phoned to say he was admitting me to the hospital immediately for surgery. "It looks like a large tumor," he said. "It may be malignant."

Dad, Mom, and my brother, Scott, met the doctors in the hospital. Despite the seriousness of the situation, my brother and I joked around like always. That helped. The morning of the operation, when the surgeon explained the procedure to us, he asked if I had any questions. I asked, "Yeah, what's for lunch?"

But deep down, I felt helpless. I was a Christian who went to church and prayed, but I never cried out to God like I did that night alone in the hospital before the surgery. *Lord Jesus, please help me.*

It didn't turn out the way we hoped. The doctor came in my room and said, "It was a malignant nine-pound tumor attached to the aorta artery. I couldn't get it all because you started to hemorrhage." My morphine drip couldn't touch the pain of hearing those words. I didn't know why God would allow this to happen. I had so much to live for.

I fought back by claiming God's promise in Jeremiah 29:11: "I have good plans for you, not plans to hurt you. I will give you hope and a good future." Hundreds prayed for me as I underwent chemotherapy and a second major surgery to remove the rest of the tumor from the aorta. Finally I could pray, *I trust you, Lord even if your answer is no.* Then I kept my eyes on the future, not on fear or death, but on hope and on life.

God's answer was yes. Now I am healthy and free to work, travel, fish, surf, and snowboard again. Each day, in some way, I feel the thankfulness I felt skiing the slopes of Banff.

ACTION STEP

THINK ABOUT THE STORY BY KENT PALMER THAT GOES WITH THIS SOUL MATTER. HAVE YOU EVER HAD A CLOSE FRIEND WHO FACED A SITUATION THIS TOUGH? HOW WOULD YOU ENCOURAGE HIM OR HER? WRITE IN YOUR OWN WORDS A LETTER OF ENCOURAGEMENT TO SOMEONE YOU KNOW WHO IS FACING A TOUGH TIME.

PRAYER

God, thank You that You have a good plan for my life. Help me remember that You are working in my life right now.

SHARING GOD'S LOVE

THE BEST WAY TO SHARE YOUR FAITH WITH OTHERS IS BY LIVING A LIFE OF OBEDIENCE AND LOVE.

You who have received so much love share it with others.
Love others the way God has loved you, with tenderness.

MOTHER TERESA

To Think About

- Has there been someone in your life who helped you have more faith in God because of the way they conducted their life?
- Do your attitudes and actions draw people closer to God or push them away?
- How can you show more love to someone who needs to know God?

LESSON FOR LIFE

PROMISES

God will...

Use your example

Daniel 12:3

1 Peter 2:12

Lead people to Himself

Psalm 78:5-7

Reward your love

Matthew 10:42

Love Each Other

BIBLE STUDY PASSAGE: 1 JOHN 2:7-10

All people will know that you are my followers if you love each other.

JOHN 13:35

When Peter wrote to a small group of Christians who were persecuted and made fun of for being Christians, he said: "Always be ready to answer everyone who asks you to explain about the hope you have" (1 Peter 3:15).

That means that all of us should be prepared to tell others how we know God is real and has made us into a new person through Jesus Christ. Have you ever thought through what you would say to someone who wants to have a personal relationship with God? Do you have a couple of Bible verses memorized that you could share with them? Would you be ready to pray with them?

But just as important as having words to say is the way we live our lives. Many people have quit going to church or attending a Christian youth group because of the bad attitudes and activities of those who call themselves Christians. Jesus tells His disciples that the easiest way people will know that they have a real and powerful relationship with God is by how they love one another.

One of the greatest and most powerful expressions of love is found in 1 Corinthians 13, where Paul says: "Love is patient and kind. Love is not jealous, it does not brag, and it is not proud. Love is not rude, is not selfish, and does not get upset with others. Love does not count up wrongs that have been done" (vv. 4-5).

How about you? Do you show love to your family through your words and your actions? To your friends? Are you helping them draw closer to God?

> But when the Holy Spirit comes to you, you will receive power. You will be my witnesses—in Jerusalem, in all of Judea, in Samaria, and in every part of the world.
> Acts 1:8

REAL LIFE

Loose Ends

AS TOLD TO LAURIE KLEIN

"Jessie," my sister quavered, "I'm scared."

"For me?" I paused in my packing. Seventeen and headed for England the next day, I was scared too.

"Yeah. And being alone with Mom. What if she gets worse?"

Living with our mother was like wearing an unraveling sweater. We'd shivered through lost jobs, broken-down cars, affairs, and desperate measures.

"What about her drinking, Jess? And those creeps who sleep over? I won't be as good a witness as you are."

"God's in control," I said. "He won't let you blow it." I had to believe this. Mom disapproved of what I was doing, big time.

"Forget this missionary thing," she'd snapped. "Go to college. Get a real job—so you don't turn out like me."

What if Mom was my true mission field?

That first night in England, exhausted and homesick, I clutched Mom's goodbye letter, all folded and wrinkly. It smelled like her. She was proud of me, it said. I lay in that foreign, ten-bed dorm room and prayed for her as I had for seven years: *Jesus, show Mom You're real.*

A week later, Mom called. "Someone invited me to church," she said. "I went alone but got lost. Then I got mad. So I figured, what the heck? I'll pray. *God,* I said, *if you're really there, like Jessie claims, show me right now where this place is, or forget it! I'm going home.* Jess, I looked up, and this big arrow sign, right in front of me, said Christian Fellowship. The pastor was a guy I went to high school with. Can you believe it?"

Although an ocean divided us, my faith leaped.

Next time she called, her life was coming apart at the seams. Fired again, depressed, and broke, she had dared God to provide money for rent. The next day, someone bought her rattletrap van for $700, exactly enough cash.

I kept praying for her. When my mission team settled in Poland, Mom e-mailed: "Dear Jessie, there's a huge change in me. I want to straighten out. I feel this peace, like maybe God's forgiven me. Now, if I can just forgive myself."

The more I prayed, the more she wrote. "Listen to this Bible verse I found for you," and "Thanks for not giving up on me," and finally, "Jess, I stopped drinking."

My mother is still sober today. God has knit our family together, woven in the loose ends. Mom says it's because I loved God enough to risk disappointing her.

"You obeyed Him anyway, Jess. You loved Him more than me. That's how I knew your God was real."

ACTION STEP

ONE OF THE SIMPLEST WAYS TO SHARE WITH SOMEONE HOW THEY CAN KNOW GOD IS CALLED THE ROMAN ROAD. ALWAYS START WITH THE FIRST VERSE LISTED. WRITE DOWN THE NEXT VERSE BESIDE IT, SO YOU KNOW WHERE TO TURN TO NEXT. REPEAT THAT WITH EACH VERSE UNTIL THE LAST ONE.

- ROMANS 1:20-21
- ROMANS 3:23
- ROMANS 5:8
- ROMANS 6:23
- ROMANS 10:9-10
- ROMANS 10:13
- ROMANS 11:36

PRAYERFULLY LOOK FOR OPPORTUNITIES TO SHARE THIS MESSAGE OF SALVATION!

PRAYER

Father, thank You for saving me.   I ask You today for the courage to tell others how good You are and the strength to share Your love.

FORGIVENESS

ONE OF THE HARDEST—AND MOST IMPORTANT—WAYS TO EXPRESS LOVE IS THROUGH FORGIVING OTHERS.

It is easier to forgive an enemy than to forgive a friend.

WILLIAM BLAKE

 To Think About

- What makes forgiving those who have hurt us so hard to do?
- What happens to us when we refuse to forgive others? What are the negative consequences?
- What happens inside of us when we do forgive others?

LESSON FOR LIFE

Walking Worthy

BIBLE STUDY PASSAGE: MATTHEW 18:21-35

As a prisoner of the Lord, I beg you to live in a way that is worthy of the people God has chosen to be his own. Always be humble and gentle. Patiently put up with each other and love each other.

EPHESIANS 4:1-2 CEV

How quick are you to ask for forgiveness and forgive others? Nothing will make your soul smaller than to refuse to ask for or grant forgiveness. Forgiveness is that wonderful expression of love that God shows us through how He treats us and commands us to practice so we don't all destroy each other!

There are a number of reasons we struggle to truly forgive others—

> • *Fairness: It's true, forgiveness isn't fair. But if we all got only what we deserve, none of us would have a chance to be at peace with God and others. God wasn't fair with us as sinners—He was merciful (Romans 5:8).*

• *Pride: We also struggle to forgive because of our pride. If we "let someone off the hook," we wonder how we can feel good about ourselves and whether others will just take advantage of us. God wants you to love and respect yourself, but He also wants you to show mercy to others like He has with you.*

• *Deep hurts: Some people have hurt us deeply—and really aren't looking for forgiveness. This makes forgiveness extremely difficult and painful. In some cases, forgiving others doesn't guarantee you will have a good relationship with that person—or should even be around them. But even if forgiveness doesn't change that person—it does change you for the better in your heart.*

The world would be a much better place if everyone sought and extended forgiveness. All you are required to do is start in your own heart!

Christ accepted you, so you should accept each other, which will bring glory to God.
Romans 15:7

 REAL LIFE

Friendship Forgives

ANNE AS TOLD TO CANDY ARRINGTON

Slamming the door, I stomped upstairs. The evening was a disaster. I wanted to be alone and stop thinking about it. I turned on the CD player, hid in the bathroom, and hoped the music would cover my sobs.

Eventually, Mom tapped on the door. She had that concerned, worried look. I could tell she wanted to ask questions. I concentrated on brushing my hair into a high ponytail, pretending to be okay.

"I'm fine. Just can't talk right now," I said, before she could ask.

It was hard to believe I'd been so excited earlier in the day. Greg*, who'd been just a friend until now, asked me to the football game. I'd been hoping for this, and finally, it happened. But things got complicated fast.

I'd already promised to do something with Kate. We used to be best friends, but recently differences in activities and friends strained our relationship. The evening was an effort at reconnecting. I was afraid if I backed out it would end our friendship. So I told Greg I'd go only if Kate could go along. That turned out to be a major mistake.

A threesome felt a little weird. By the time we got to the stadium, I knew why. Kate was already flirting. It made me sick. And worse, Greg seemed to enjoy the attention! The more I watched, the madder I got.

Now my chin quivered and I kept sniffing. Mom was still standing there, so I blurted out, "She stole Greg from me! She knows I like him and is deliberately trying to hurt me. Now they're going out. If she hadn't gone with us, this would never have happened! I was trying to be her friend. She stabbed me in the back."

"I know this hurts," said Mom. "You have every reason to be angry, but you know the struggles in Kate's life. Sometimes when people are insecure, they react by hurting others. It made Kate feel loved and important to take Greg away from you. It will be really hard, but could you forgive her?"

"She'll never admit she's done anything wrong or say she's sorry," I said.

"Probably not and that's when it's most difficult to forgive, but unforgiveness ruins relationships. Learning to extend the gift of forgiveness to someone who hurts you, whether they apologize or not, will benefit you for the rest of your life."

I didn't want to hear that. I wanted to stay mad. But by the next day, I knew what I should do. I kept thinking about how Jesus forgives even when we don't deserve it and remembering all the times I'd let Him down. If He could forgive me, I could forgive Kate. It's still hard not to be mad. What she did changes everything about my relationship with her and with Greg. It'll take a while for me to trust her again, but I know God is pleased because I chose to forgive.

I'm not going to let Kate's actions hurt me twice by choosing to live with anger.

*Names have been changed

ACTION STEP

IS THERE SOMEONE SPECIAL IN YOUR LIFE WHO HAS HURT YOU? ARE YOU STILL HARBORING BITTERNESS? HAVE YOU WITHHELD FORGIVENESS? WRITE A LETTER TO THAT PERSON OFFERING THEM GOD'S LOVE AND YOUR FORGIVENESS. YOU DON'T HAVE TO SEND IT TO THE PERSON RIGHT AWAY, BUT MIGHT HOLD ONTO IT AS YOU PRAY FOR GOD TO GIVE YOU A HEART OF LOVE TOWARD THEM.

PRAYER

Dear Heavenly Father, thank You for the forgiveness You continually offer me. Please heal my heart as I choose to forgive those who have hurt me today.

PARENTS

NO MATTER HOW IMPERFECT YOUR PARENTS MAY SEEM, LOVING AND RESPECTING THEM IS THE ONLY ROUTE TO BLESSINGS.

When I was a boy of 14, my father was so ignorant I could hardly stand to have the old man around. But when I got to be 21, I was astonished at how much the old man had learned in seven years.

MARK TWAIN

 TO THINK ABOUT

- How is your relationship with your parents?
- What are the positive dynamics? Are there negatives?
- Are you grateful for your parents? Do you show love and respect? Do you honor them?

LESSON FOR LIFE

PROMISES

God will...

Bless you as you honor

your parents

Exodus 20:12

Be your Father

Psalm 68:5

Help and forgive you

Psalm 86:5

Heal you

Jeremiah 17:14

Show It

BIBLE STUDY PASSAGE: EPHESIANS 4:17-32

My children, we should love people not only with words and talk, but by our actions and true caring.

1 JOHN 3:18

Have you ever noticed that we tend to be at our very best—charming, kind, considerate—with casual acquaintances and even complete strangers? And then we act our absolute worst—rude, impatient, moody, ungrateful—with those who are closest to us?

Are you talking about me or my parents?

And it's not just teens! Parents, husbands, wives, and sons and daughters, all fall into the trap of taking for granted those who love them most. The good news is that it doesn't have to be that way! In fact, there are two simple steps that will cure the majority of family conflicts—and make any family stronger.

The first step is cultivating a spirit of gratitude. When was the last time you felt thankful for your parents? (And said, "Thanks, Mom.") The issue isn't whether your parents are perfect. Your parents might be divorced or argue so much with each other that your home is filled with stress. You can still find reasons for gratitude—even if the only reason is that they are the parents God gave to you.

The second step to improving family relationships is simply demonstrating your love. How can you show your mom, your dad, through actions that you truly love them? The Apostle James said that faith without works is dead (James 2:17), and in the same way love without actions is empty.

What will you "say" to your parents today?

Honor your father and your mother so that you will live a long time in the land that the Lord your God is going to give you.

Exodus 20:12

REAL LIFE

The Christmas I Grew Up

TERRENCE CONKLIN

It was 4 AM on Christmas Eve. My father was lying in my parents' bedroom with his cardiothoracic leggings on, his heart pillow to his chest for when he coughed, and wrapped in four or five blankets to keep him warm. He was recovering from surgery after his recent heart attack.

My little brother was sleeping on the couch and waiting for Santa to come. He hoped to "catch him in the act" this year. This was hardly unusual for this particular night of the year, if you overlooked the fact that downstairs, two other creatures were stirring—my mother and myself.

With my father laid up after his brush with death, my mother was left to handle Christmas all by herself. And at thirteen, I was hit with the hard truth about Santa Claus.

Everything seemed completely wrong and unfair. I watched my mother wrapping last-minute gifts, placing on the tags, and carrying them up the stairs in exhaustion—of course, tiptoeing past my sleeping brother.

This had not exactly been what I had in mind for my Christmas break. I was the usual selfish teenager, who had spent the last week doing nothing but trying to get out of holiday chores. After all, I was supposed to be on vacation!

As if all of that weren't bad enough, that night I was dragged to the holiday services at church. But as I watched my mother, face on, from my position in the youth group choir loft, something changed. I saw her in our familiar pew, sitting there without my father. She was struggling to keep my brother from wiggling. She closed her eyes in a deep prayer, and tears began to flow down her cheeks. And in that moment, as if for the first time ever, I heard the commandment: "Honor your father and your mother so that you will live a long time in the land that the Lord your God is going to give you."

That night my mother and I stayed up into the wee hours of the morning, stuffing stockings, filling the empty space under the tree, and trying not to trigger the train set that now encircled the tree stand and wake my sleeping brother.

Seeing how much my mother put into Christmas with an out-of-work, desperately ill husband and two young children, made me begin to respect her. I rushed to do anything she asked, and did not grumble in my cranky, "teenage" way.

I wanted to honor both of my parents, always, and I would try to teach my brother to do the same. Especially when "Mrs. Claus" needed help.

The Christmas lights shone on my mother's face as we placed the last gift under the tree. But that Christmas I received a greater gift: I had learned honor and obedience, and I hoped we would all live long in the Lord.

ACTION STEP

OFTEN WE WONDER WHY PEOPLE—ESPECIALLY PARENTS—DON'T UNDER-
STAND US, BUT NEVER TAKE THE TIME TO TRY AND UNDERSTAND OTHERS.
GROW IN YOUR APPRECIATION OF YOUR PARENTS BY GETTING TO KNOW THEM
BETTER. MAKE A SHORT LIST OF QUESTIONS—AND INTERVIEW THEM AS IF YOU
WERE A REPORTER. MAKE NOTES IN YOUR JOURNAL AND USE THEM TO BETTER
UNDERSTAND WHERE YOUR PARENTS ARE COMING FROM. QUESTIONS MIGHT
INCLUDE: WHAT WAS IT LIKE GROWING UP WHEN YOU WERE A KID? WHO WAS
YOUR BEST FRIEND? FAVORITE TEACHER? WHAT WAS YOUR BEST MOMENT?
TOUGHEST MOMENT? WHEN DID YOU BEGIN TO "GROW UP"?

PRAYER

Dear Father God—
Teach me and help me to show love and honor to my parents. No matter what
happens in my life, thank You that You are my Heavenly Father and I can
always count on You.

GREED AND MATERIALISM

A DANGER TO YOUR SOUL IN OUR PROSPEROUS SOCIETY IS TO VALUE POSSESSIONS MORE THAN PEOPLE—AND MORE THAN A RELATIONSHIP WITH GOD.

He is rich or poor according to what he is,
not according to what he has.

HENRY WARD BEECHER

 TO THINK ABOUT

- Does your community have a blend of people with different financial circumstances—from rich to poor?
- What are the problems with having too little money? What are the problems with having too much money?
- Do you ever struggle with greed and materialism?

LESSON FOR LIFE

PROMISES

God will...

Make your life great, no
matter what your
circumstances are
Philippians 4:11-13

Give you joy
Proverbs 15:15

Provide for your needs
1 Timothy 6:17

Give you good things
Ecclesiastes 2:24
Psalm 16:6

First Things First

BIBLE STUDY PASSAGE: MATTHEW 6:25-34

*The thing you should want most is God's kingdom and
doing what God wants.   Then all these other things you
need will be given to you.*

MATTHEW 6:33

When a young man came to visit Jesus, he asked what he
must do to become one of Jesus' followers.   Jesus told the man
that he must give away all his possessions and join Him in His
ministry right now.   The young man wanted to be a disciple,
but he was very rich and liked his wealth, so he sadly walked
away from Jesus (Matthew 19:22).

To become a true disciple—one who follows—Jesus, do all
of us need to give away our possessions and be poor?   Do you?
The answer is simple.   If Jesus asks you to give everything, do
it.   If He doesn't, don't!   But be aware that all of us are
required to make Jesus the first priority in our lives.   He must
be more important than possessions.   As He said to His disciples: "The thing you should want most is God's kingdom and
doing what God wants.   Then all these other things you need

will be given to you" (Matthew 6:33).

Some of the problems that occur when we make money and things the highest values in our lives include—

- *We begin to drift away from God because of distractions.*
- *We lose a passion to serve God because we become selfish.*
- *We don't love others the same way because of greed and envy.*
- *We become unhappy and ungrateful because we focus on what we don't have instead of what we do have.*

Is it wrong to have nice clothes and shoes that are in style? Is it wrong to hope for a cool car to drive to school?   Is it wrong to buy new video games and electronic equipment?   Is it wrong to go out to eat at nice places with friends?

The answers are between you and God.   But what matters most for your soul is that you love Him first and others second.

Keep your lives free from the love of money, and be satisfied with what you have. God has said, "I will never leave you; I will never forget you." Hebrews 13:5

REAL LIFE

My Mansion

CLAY MCGUIRE

"Mom, do we have to drive this car?" I asked for the umpteenth time. Our car was a huge clunker, in an out-of-date color and style.

There were two kinds of students in my school: the wealthy and those like me, whose families struggled to pay tuition. We weren't poor. We lived in a nice two-story house, but, compared to my friends' homes, it looked like a doll-house.

Mom would smile, "We'd rather drive old cars and live in a smaller house to be able to give you a great education in a school where faith is also important." Usually she would add, "We really are rich compared to most people in the world." I didn't want to hear that. Instead I thought about the day a friend turned sixteen and got a new car delivered to her at school.

I wanted a good education, but I didn't get into all the extra-curricular activities at my school. I did like participating in church youth events and service projects. "You really have a tender heart, Clay," Mom encouraged.

A family from our church moved to Honduras to start a medical clinic, and when they returned home to gather equipment, my family helped pack their trunks. An idea was born in my mind and slowly grew. That summer I made up my mind and announced, "Mom and Dad, I want to live with Doris and Robert and work in Honduras for a few months."

Everyone agreed, and soon I found myself bumping along in a rickety bus, wedged in between Hondurans and crates of chickens. They smiled and were helpful, even though I didn't speak Spanish.

I loved being there, helping at the clinic and working with a Christian school and orphanage. After returning home I knew I wanted to go back to Honduras; I liked doing something I considered more meaningful than clubs and sports.

"Mom and Dad," I begged, "please let me go back. Doris will home-school me for a semester, along with Robert Junior." To my surprise, they agreed!

I quickly learned more Spanish. Then Robert and I were trusted with extra responsibilities, meeting groups that came down from the States, accompanying them from the capital to the clinic, and leading them in various work projects.

Soon we were allowed to drive across rain-swollen creeks to the places roads ended. From there we rode horses or hiked to more remote villages. The doctors allowed us to help treat cuts and sew up machete wounds.

Life was simple. We ate crackers and drank water we carried with us, or enjoyed beans, rice, and coffee with the villagers. We slept under the stars or sometimes in a hammock in a room with a dirt floor.

All too soon it was time to return to my world. As we rounded the curve in our neighborhood I felt like Saul when the scales fell from his eyes. I stared at our house in total awe. I finally got it! She just smiled when I said, "Mom, we live in a mansion!"

ACTION STEP

GO THROUGH ALL YOUR CLOTHES AND OTHER POSSESSIONS AND PULL OUT
EVERYTHING YOU HAVEN'T USED IN THE PAST YEAR. SELL IT ON EBAY OR AT A
GARAGE SALE AND DONATE THE MONEY TO A WORTHY MISSION IN YOUR AREA.

PRAYER

*Father, I know that You love me and want good things for me. Help me put my
trust in You, not in what I have.*

SMALL MIRACLES

WHEN LIFE GETS PARTICULARLY TOUGH, KEEP YOUR EYES AND HEART OPEN FOR GOD'S SMALL MIRACLES.

Just as there comes a warm sunbeam into every cottage window, so comes a love born of God's care for every separate need.

NATHANIEL HAWTHORNE

 To Think About

- Have you ever experienced an incredible moment when you just knew God was doing something special just for you?
- Do you believe in miracles and divine intervention in your life?
- Do you go throughout your day with a sense of God's love for you?

LESSON FOR LIFE

PROMISES

God will...

Meet all your needs

Philippians 4:19

Hear your prayers

1 Peter 3:12

Be with you

Isaiah 43:2

Put you in a loving body

of believers

1 Peter 1:22

Tender Mercies

BIBLE STUDY PASSAGE: JEREMIAH 31:1-20

Let us, then, feel very sure that we can come before God's throne where there is grace.   There we can receive mercy and grace to help us when we need it.

HEBREWS 4:16

When we get to the end of our own strength, realizing that we need God to make it in life and keep our soul tender and true, it's good to remember—

- *God sent a rainbow to Noah as a symbol that His love for man would never waver (Genesis 9:14-15).*
- *God spoke to Moses in a burning bush (Exodus 3:2-6) and parted the waters of the sea with His breath to free the Israelite people (Exodus 14:21).*
- *God allowed a young shepherd boy to conquer a mighty warrior with only a sling shot and a single stone (1 Samuel 17:49).*
- *Jesus healed a blind man (Mark 8:22-25), a person with leprosy (Matthew 8:2-3), a man who had never walked*

(Matthew 9:2-7), and even raised a young girl from death to life (Luke 8:51-55).

· *The Holy Spirit came upon the followers of Jesus so they could proclaim God's love in languages they'd never spoken before (Acts 2:4-8).*

God is at work in our world—and in your life. Sometimes all we need is to open our eyes to see His tender mercies in our lives. Look around. You just might see a miracle today.

Give all your worries to him, because he cares about you.

1 Peter 5:7

43

REAL LIFE

The Necklace

JENNA MITCHELL

It was the winter of my sophomore year of high school, and I was already counting the days until summer vacation.   Every morning, I dressed for school, tested my blood, took my shot, ate, ran out the door, and headed to my first class, half wishing I didn't have to go to school that day.

It had been a difficult year for me.   Being at a new school is challenging for most kids.   It didn't help any that I had to monitor my diabetes and live with other health-related issues.   Regardless, I attended class four periods a day and met with a home schoolteacher two days a week.   This gave me a full class load.

The highlight of my day was choir class.   There I felt accepted.

Half of the girls in the choir were typical—the other half was made up of girls with special needs.   Though our looks and abilities varied, we all loved lip gloss, new clothes, and singing!

One day, our class periods ran short so the entire school could gather at the amphitheater for the "Holiday Wish Fairy Assembly."   For a moment the only wish I had was that I was back at the Christian high school I had attended my freshman year.   How I wished that it didn't have to close!

Since I had never been to a "Holiday Wish Fairy Assembly" before, I had no idea what to expect.   I sat back and waited for it to be over.   The assembly began with announcements, and then the "wishing" began.   One by one, members of the ASB cabinet called various students to the stage. Each student made a wish. One wished for a car, another a dog, and the dreaming went on.

This is a dumb assembly! I thought.

Soon all eyes were on Elizabeth, a girl from my choir. *What's she doing up there?* I wondered. *For a girl with special needs—she sure has guts!*

Elizabeth stepped in front of the microphone. Without a tremble in her voice she began to talk. "My wish today is that I could give Jenna Mitchell a present in front of the school."

Jenna Mitchell? That's me! My heart began to pound.

Within seconds, someone announced, "Would Jenna Mitchell please come up to meet Elizabeth?"

Without thinking I rose to my feet and began the long walk to the stage. With the entire school watching, I smiled at Elizabeth, then stood by her side.

Elizabeth began her short monologue which she had rehearsed several times. "I want to thank Jenna for being my best friend at school, and I want to give her this necklace."

Extending her hand toward mine, Elizabeth gave me a small gold box tied with a matching ribbon. As the students watched, I thanked Elizabeth and gave her a hug.

With tears in my eyes I returned to my seat. Then I realized I did have friends at my new school. I also had a "best friend"—one who understood how it felt to be different, who knew what it was like to have special needs, and who, like me, loved to sing!

I will always treasure that little necklace as a gift from Elizabeth and from God.

ACTION STEP

ONE OF THE KEY WORDS IN THE BIBLE IS "REMEMBER." WE ARE TO
REMEMBER GOD'S WORKS, HIS MERCY, HIS FAITHFULNESS. SOMETIMES WE
FORGET ALL GOD HAS DONE FOR US.

FIND SOME TIME TO WRITE DOWN THE GRACIOUS DEEDS THE LORD HAS DONE
FOR YOU SINCE YOU'VE BEEN WALKING WITH HIM.

TUCK YOUR "STORY" INTO YOUR BIBLE, AND LOOK AT IT AGAIN FROM TIME TO
TIME. THIS MIGHT ALSO BE A GREAT TIME TO START A SPIRITUAL JOURNAL IF
YOU HAVEN'T ALREADY DONE SO—A DAY-TO-DAY RECORD OF YOUR LIFE WITH
GOD.

PRAYER

*Dear Heavenly Father, thank You that being Your child means seeing Your
comfort and provision in every detail of my life. Thank You for Your goodness.*

LIFE CHANGE

GOD IS ABLE TO CHANGE A PERSON FROM THE INSIDE OUT.

Salvation is not something that is done for you but something that happens within you.

ALBERT W. PALMER

TO THINK ABOUT

- ☛ Do you truly believe that people can change for the better?
- ☛ Have you ever written someone off because of past mistakes?
- ☛ Have you ever been tempted to give up on yourself?

LESSON FOR LIFE

PROMISES

God will...

Give you a new heart
Ezekiel 36:26-27

Colossians 3:10

Forgive you
Ephesians 1:7

Guide your path
Proverbs 4:11-12

Do We Really Have a Choice?

BIBLE STUDY PASSAGE: LUKE 19:2-8

You have begun to live the new life, in which you are being made new and are becoming like the One who made you This new life brings you the true knowledge of God.

COLOSSIANS 3:10

For centuries, people have debated what makes a person who they are—are we born the way we are, or do we become this way through the things that happen to us?

Some psychologists believe that everything a person does is determined by the shaping influences in their lives like parents and life experiences—some go so far as to say that once a person is five, their personality is shaped and really can't be changed.

Other people think that we are primarily a product of genetics, that our behavior and attitudes follow from the way we are "wired." Common expressions of this idea would include: "I can't help it, it's just the way I was born"; or "a leopard can't change his spots"; or "the nut doesn't fall far from the tree."

48

Though our genes and life experiences have a huge impact on us, aren't you glad that there is a miraculous, powerful God who is able to change even the most stubborn, damaged, sinful heart? Paul goes so far as to say, "If anyone belongs to Christ, there is a new creation. The old things have gone; everything is made new!" (2 Corinthians 5:17). After a change of heart at the moment of conversion, God isn't finished with us, either. Paul says: "We all show the Lord's glory, and we are being changed to be like him" (2 Corinthians 3:18).

But you don't understand how I've been brought up. You don't know the mistakes I've made. You don't understand how hard it is for me to stop doing some things.

With grace, with faith, with the help of godly friends, you can say along with Paul: "Forgetting the past and straining toward what is ahead, I keep trying to reach the goal and get the prize for which God called me through Christ to the life above" (Philippians 3:13-14). Because of His forgiving, life-changing power, God's ultimate concern with your life is not where you've been, but where you are going.

Though your sins are like scarlet, they can be as white as snow. Though your sins are deep red, they can be white like wool.

Isaiah 1:18

REAL LIFE

Nothing Funny About It

AS TOLD TO LINDA HENSON

I grew up on the south side of Chicago, which can be a rough place for teenagers. I knew I was destined to be a leader in my neighborhood—it was easy for me to gain a following. I wasn't in a gang; I was forming my own!

I liked nice things and having a roll of money in my pocket, so I was an easy sell for some "mob" connected guys. They would come to me and tell me which car to steal. They told me to drive it into Lake Michigan; they would collect the insurance and pay me a good fee. Nothing to it. If I got caught, I would just be a "joyriding teenager" and they would deny ever knowing me.

The money bought me things that impressed my friends and supported my drug involvement. And so we partied. Partying was all I wanted to do. Most of the time, I used my quick wit to entertain and become the center of attention. The favorite entertainment was when I did my "act," mimicking the most popular TV evangelists of the day. I could "preach" up a storm. The guys would roll on the floor laughing at my renditions (though I wasn't sure I would be as funny if they were sober).

My mother was a "Jesus-loving" Catholic. The more partying I did, the more she prayed. I didn't know it at the time, but even my future mother-in-law was praying for me, even though she didn't know me.

One night I came in from a party and found Mom with a group of her praying friends.   When she saw the state I was in, she grabbed a bottle of "holy water" and threw it on me, and all of those ladies chased me down, laying their hands on me.   They prayed and told the devil he had to go in Jesus' name.   I thought it was hilarious and started laughing till I fell on the floor and couldn't get away from them.

One night, one of the guys saw my "act" and afterwards said, "Jorje, there's a church in Homewood that would give you some great material for your stories. Let's go over there Friday night."   That sounded good to me.   My old stories were getting a little stale.

On Friday night, we slipped into the back pew, and all through the service, I elbowed my friend in the ribs with a wink signaling a good story for our next party.

I don't know what happened, but all of a sudden, it wasn't funny anymore. The preacher was somehow relating to the emptiness I felt on the inside.   When he invited people to come and repent, I came running down the aisle.

My life was instantly changed from the inside out—from that moment on there were no more drugs, no more parties.   I kept coming to the evangelist's meetings and began to bring my friends.

Two weeks later, I enrolled in a Bible college.   And I've never looked back.

ACTION STEP

IDENTIFY A NEW ATTITUDE OR A NEW HABIT YOU WANT TO DEVELOP IN YOUR LIFE. OR, IDENTIFY AN OLD ATTITUDE OR AN OLD HABIT YOU WANT ELIMINATED FROM YOUR LIFE. COMMIT THIS CHANGE OF HEART TO GOD AND ASK HIM TO DO A SPECIAL WORK IN YOU. YOU MIGHT EXPERIENCE AN INSTANTANEOUS, MIRACULOUS CHANGE—OR YOU MIGHT EXPERIENCE A GRADUAL GROWTH AND GRACE. EITHER WAY, DON'T FORGET THAT GOD IS THE SOURCE OF YOUR STRENGTH.

PRAYER

Thank You, O God, for making me a new person through Your Son Jesus. I ask You to continue and complete the good work You started in me.

DETERMINATION

WHEN LIFE IS DIFFICULT, WE COME OUT VICTORIOUS THROUGH FAITH, COURAGE, PERSEVERANCE—AND JOY.

Walk boldly and wisely.
There is a hand above that will help you on.

PHILIP JAMES BAILEY

 To Think About

- What is one thing you have that you really had to work hard and long for?
- Did your efforts make the accomplishment more valuable?
- What is something that will come to you in the future only if you persevere?

LESSON FOR LIFE

PROMISES

God will...

Strengthen you
Psalm 138:3

Comfort you
2 Thessalonians 2:16-17

Use your difficulties to
make you stronger
Romans 5:3

Use your difficulties to
glorify himself
1 Corinthians 1:27

Joy in a Jail Cell

BIBLE STUDY PASSAGE: PHILIPPIANS 4:10-19

I do not mean that I am already as God wants me to be. I have not yet reached that goal, but I continue trying to reach it and to make it mine.

PHILIPPIANS 3:12

Philippians is known as a book about joy—some form of the word "joy" appears in nine verses in this relatively short letter—despite being written by Paul from a Roman prison. In both his words and his actions, Paul asks us to be glad in spite of suffering (ch. 1), in the midst of humble service (ch. 2), and in the face of fear and anxiety (ch. 4).

But is it practical to think we can rejoice in any situation? When a parent dies? When a friendship crumbles? When a family member hurts us? Is it even healthy to find joy in such times?

Note that Paul does not say to be happy because of hardship; he says rejoice despite and in the midst of pain. Paul doesn't call us to wish for hardship and pain in our lives, but he does call us to be overcomers in all circumstances.

And Paul knows what he's talking about. This is the man who was stoned and beaten (Acts 14:19, 21:30-32), shipwrecked (Acts 27:39), suffered from a painful physical sickness (Galatians 4:13-14), lived with the guilt of being a persecutor of innocent people in his past (Acts 22:4), and was imprisoned and sentenced to death for his faith (Acts 16:22-24). But like the Energizer Bunny, he just kept on going and going and going. Why? How? He was a man of joy.

Paul's final message to the Philippians concerns the way this church cared for him during his trials. He says that their gifts and compassion were "a sweet-smelling sacrifice offered to God, who accepts that sacrifice and is pleased with it" (4:18). Helping someone else persevere is a fragrant, pleasing prayer to God!

Yes, life can be difficult. But even in the midst of suffering we can stand firm—and help others to do the same—as we joyfully keep going with God's help.

Did you know that perseverance and failure cannot coexist? Why? Failure only happens when you quit. Remember, whether you're dealing with a relationship, a spiritual issue, or a personal soul, as long as you keep trying, you are in the game.

You know that these troubles test your faith, and this will give you patience.

James 1:3

REAL LIFE

Anissa's Answer

AS TOLD TO SUSANNE SCHEPPMANN

My new coach's eyes questioned me as he grasped the soccer mitt. I attempted to jerk my hand away, but could not wiggle out of his grip. As we stood facing each other in front of the goalie net, I knew what was coming before he spoke.

"Anissa, what is the hard lump I feel inside of this mitt?"

"It's my hand."

He frowned disbelievingly at me. He began to speak, but I interrupted.

"Actually, it's not a hand. Because I don't have hands. I was born without hands."

Letting go of me, he asked, "What in the world are you talking about, Anissa?"

With my eyes cast down to the ground, I pushed off both mitts. I felt his startled stare as two fleshy stumps with three stubby appendages appeared before him. A rush of embarrassment flooded my face as I heard him gasp.

"I don't understand. What happened?"

Pushing my blond hair back from my eyes I stared defiantly at him. Replying, "I told you—I was born without hands. It's called amniotic band syndrome. My hands got tangled in coarse fibers in my mom's uterus. The dental floss-like fibers cut off my hands."

I continued now pleading, "But Coach, I can still be the goalie. My hands don't affect the way I play soccer. I been playing since I was four. That's ten years of soccer! Coach Raft knew about it. If he were here, he would tell you I could help us win today."

He squared his shoulders as a look of stubborn resolve swept across his lean face. His dark eyes focused somewhere above my head. Without looking at me he said, "Anissa, I had no idea. You know this game is too important for us to lose. If we lose, then we won't go to the championship game today. If you want to help the team, go sit on the sideline."

I could feel the tears running down my cheeks as I ran after him shouting, "Coach, please!"

"Anissa, we'll talk about this later. Not now."

The coach had questioned me and judged me as incompetent to finish the game. It was always the same—questions and judgments about my hands.

Now I asked, *Why God? Oh, please let me play!* as I sat and watched the team play the game I longed to play.

I was still thinking about how hard it was to prove myself when suddenly and unexpectedly, I heard my coach holler, "Anissa, get in the game! We need you to make the winning goal! Hurry!"

As I turned and raced onto the grassy field, I realized suddenly my questions might not ever be completely answered. Why was I born without hands? I don't know, but I do have two feet to kick a soccer goal. People might initially assume I can't compete in life, but I'll just have to show them differently. And with the help of the God who created me, I will!

ACTION STEP

IF LIFE IS MORE LIKE A MARATHON THAN A SPRINT, WHY NOT WALK OR RUN YOUR OWN PERSONAL MARATHON TODAY? NO, YOU DON'T HAVE TO COVER TWENTY-SIX MILES ON FOOT, BUT PLOT OUT A NICE, LONG COURSE, AND SPEND THE TIME TALKING TO GOD ABOUT THE VARIOUS CHALLENGES YOU ARE FACING NOW, THANKING HIM FOR HIS HELP EACH STEP OF YOUR JOURNEY AHEAD, AND PRAISING HIM THAT HE LOVES YOU AND CARES ABOUT ALL AREAS OF YOUR LIFE.

PRAYER

Thank You, Heavenly Father, that no matter what challenges I face today and tomorrow, You provide me with the physical, emotional, and spiritual resources that I need.

GOD CAN USE YOU

EVEN WHEN WE ARE UNCERTAIN ABOUT OUR ABILITIES, GOD HAS CONFIDENCE IN US AND CAN DO GREAT THINGS THROUGH US.

It is not the possession of extraordinary gifts
that makes extraordinary usefulness, but the dedication
of what we have to the serve of God.

FREDERICK WILLIAM ROBERTSON

TO THINK ABOUT

- 🔑 Have you ever felt called by God to help someone or do something good but were too afraid to try?
- 🔑 Do most of your friends have a healthy self-esteem, or are they good at faking it?
- 🔑 What is something great you would like to accomplish in life? Have you talked to God about this?

LESSON FOR LIFE

PROMISES

God will...

Reward your efforts

1 Corinthians 3:8

Prepare you for good works

Ephesians 2:10

Delight in you

Psalm 147:11

Deal with you according to your heart

1 Samuel 16:7

My God Shall Supply

BIBLE STUDY PASSAGE: EXODUS 4:1-17

But Moses said to the Lord, "Please, Lord, I have never been a skilled speaker. Even now, after talking to you, I cannot speak well. I speak slowly and can't find the best words."

EXODUS 4:10

We live in a dog-eat-dog world. It sometimes seems like only the most athletic, best looking, and most near perfect get noticed. Many of us question our abilities and are fearful about testing our wings and attempting all that God has called us to do.

If you ever struggle with healthy self-confidence, note that one of the greatest leaders in all of history, Moses, had the same hang-up. When God called him to lead the children of Israel out of Egyptian bondage, Moses was full of excuses. *They won't listen to me. I stutter. Send my brother.* Maybe it was the trauma of separation from his parents as a baby and being adapted into a "foreign" culture. Maybe it was the guilt of things he'd done in his youth or being raised as a prince while his own family served as slaves.   Whatever the reasons, Moses had deep fears about whether he was good enough.

But God was patient with him and didn't demand that Moses work on his speech or schmooze with the right people to make him a more effective leader.   When Moses trusted God and stepped out on faith to confront the Pharaoh and help forge a free nation, he took to heart God's promise to him: "I will help you speak, and I will teach you what to say" (Exodus 4:12).

Yes, we should continually improve ourselves.   It's good to strive for excellence in our lives.   But we shouldn't forget that God often gives us things to accomplish that are beyond our abilities and can use us no matter what seems to stand in the way.   No matter how much "work" you think you need right now, be assured that God can use you just as you are.

God has made us what we are.   In Christ Jesus, God made us to do good works, which God planned in advance for us to live our lives doing.
Ephesians 2:10

REAL LIFE

Don't Wait to Make a Difference

AS TOLD TO KATHRYN LAY

When I first arrived in America, I couldn't speak English, but four years later, God helped me to be a translator for other Bosnian refugees.

I found Christ in Bosnia when I was a young child, and found my future in America in high school. One December, I left war-torn Bosnia with my parents and three younger brothers. We spent one month in a United Nations camp in Croatia before being transferred to a refugee camp. After many medical exams and a lot of paperwork, months later we were on our way to America.

Soon I began attending ESL (English as a Second Language) classes at a nearby church. As I improved my English, I began serving God by helping the leaders of the school.

I'd only been in America two months when a Bosnian woman asked me to translate for her when she went to a local charity organization to get help in finding a job. I was scared, but I helped her, and soon I was asked more and more often for translation help.

I began working at a hospital as their Bosnian translator. Although I as a high school student cared for my non-English speaking family, I was on call twenty-four hours a day, seven days a week for the hospital. Soon I was translating for hospitals, the police department, businesses, and charity groups.

God gave me the chance to help others and share my belief in Christ.

You never know what the outcome of each situation will be. One night, a detective I was working with on a criminal case called me at work to say that a Bosnian woman had been hit by a car. The accident happened in front of my apartment, and they wanted me to translate.

I sensed God's urging to call home and learned from my father that it had been my mother who was hit. When I got there, I was terrified, but was able to help and comfort my mother.

I am the only Christian in my family and a rarity in the Muslim world of my people. I hope that my life and love for God is a beacon of light in a dark world.

Through my work as a translator, volunteer work in the church office, time helping the ESL ministry, and working on the school newspaper, I know I am following God. I have lived through many lifetimes in nineteen years, experiencing war and loss, hope in a new land, the love of God, and a way to minister through it all.

God fills me so full every time I serve people and the Lord.

ACTION STEP

WHAT IS ONE THING WANT TO DO, BUT AREN'T QUITE SURE YOU CAN? TALK TO SOMEONE YOU'VE NEVER MET BEFORE? SING OR PLAY AN INSTRUMENT WITH YOUR CHURCH WORSHIP TEAM? DETERMINE ONE STEP YOU CAN TAKE FORWARD, AND PRAYERFULLY GO FOR IT THIS WEEK!

PRAYER

Lord, thank You that You use us to do big things in the world. Help me hear Your voice and do all that You've called me to do.

THE FUTURE

GOD HAS A WONDERFUL PLAN IN STORE FOR YOU—A PLAN THAT BEGINS TODAY!

*The uncertainties of the present always give way
to the enchanted possibilities of the future.*

GELSEY KIRKLAND

 To Think About

- 🗝 Does thinking about the future cause you to feel hopeful, or fearful?
- 🗝 Have you ever sensed God leading you to take a new path that will change your future?
- 🗝 Are you trusting your future to God right now?

LESSON FOR LIFE

PROMISES

God will...

Guide you
Isaiah 58:11

Work out His
plan for your life
Psalm 138:8

Be with you
Isaiah 43:2

A Future and a Hope

BIBLE STUDY PASSAGE: JOHN 10:10-16

"I say this because I know what I am planning for you,"
says the Lord. "I have good plans for you, not plans to hurt
you. I will give you hope and a good future."

JEREMIAH 29:11

Jeremiah is known as the "weeping prophet" because he cried so much.   He felt such grief for his people.   Imagine losing absolutely everything you hold dear—your family, home, country, church, and maybe even your faith.   Jeremiah was devastated by what had happened to his people.   King Nebuchadnezzar had conquered the Kingdom of Judah, destroying the walls of Jerusalem and the temple built by Solomon.   The strongest and most educated youth were led as captives to serve the conquering king.   They left behind the city they loved, smoldering in ruins.

This young man of God preached to the Hebrew exiles, who now lived in the foreign country of Babylon, along the banks of the Tigris River.

The Israelites had lost all hope.   How could they think of

themselves as God's chosen people under such circumstances?

But even in the middle of all this hopelessness, this young prophet, Jeremiah, called to speak for God at an early age, dried his eyes and boldly proclaimed a new promise—that God had a future filled with hope for these people. That promise did come true for the Hebrew children, and the promise still echoes and holds true for God's people today.

You may feel comfortable about the future—or you may be anxious about all the decisions you face and where they might take you. College? Career? Friendships? Dating?

No matter what your situation, the truth is that God created you for His glory (Isaiah 43:7) and gave you special gifts. Just as He had a plan for His people thousands of years ago, He has a plan for you—a good, pleasing, and perfect plan. And He is trustworthy to make that plan happen, no matter where we are on the journey.

The Lord says, "I will make you wise and show you where to go. I will guide you and watch over you."
Psalm 32:8

REAL LIFE

Ministry—Me?

ANNA FOREHAND AS TOLD TO JESSICA INMAN

The red numbers of my alarm clock taunted me. I'd been in bed for an hour, and I just couldn't sleep. Maybe I drank one too many Grasshoppers at the coffeehouse.

Maybe it was something else that was keeping me up. Something hadn't felt right lately. I hadn't felt as close to God as I used to—I just wasn't feeling it the same way.

It wasn't doing me any good to just stare at the dark ceiling. I flipped on the light and found my CD player under some clothes. I sat and listened to music, daydreaming about what I wanted to do when I "grew up." It was down to veterinarian and lawyer.

As I rehearsed possible scenarios about treating dog lung cancer and winning landmark cases, a thought kept circling me: youth ministry. I pushed it aside a couple times, but finally I stopped and thought about it.

Youth ministry would be a ton of fun. I loved going to youth group—I was a church rat, always at drama practice or worship team practice or small group meetings. I also loved music and could see myself leading students in worship. Still, was I hearing right? I prayed, *God, is this really what You want me to do? Or is this just a job I chose because I think it'd be fun?*

I had to talk to someone. The next time I saw my prayer partner, I told her what I'd been thinking.   Mandee was so supportive—she encouraged me and told me she'd be praying for me.   And I talked to a couple youth leaders at my church, who really encouraged me.   One said he'd pray for me, and the other gave me a book to read.

Then I went to a big youth service with students and pastors from my part of the state.   During worship, I went down to the altar to pray—was I experiencing a "call"?

A youth pastor in my city whom I knew really well came and talked with me.   Something she said stayed with me: "If this is for the good of God, then there should be no doubt in your mind that it's from Him."

Over the next few weeks, I thought about it.   And I do think God is giving me a heart for student ministry.

I'm not sure what will happen in the coming years.   I may be a volunteer youth leader the rest of my life, or maybe help with leading worship.   Who knows?   The world is wide.

Now, every time I set foot in church, I'm thinking, *What can I do to make people feel welcome, to feel like they matter, to feel like they belong in church?*

No matter what the future holds, I can begin right now to be God's hands and feet to students.

ACTION STEP

IN A JOURNAL OR A BLANK SHEET OF PAPER, WRITE A LIST OF NINE THINGS YOU WOULD LOVE TO BE PART OF YOUR FUTURE. NUMBER EACH OF THEM AND THEN WRITE DOWN THE NUMBER "10." NEXT TO THAT, WRITE, "WHATEVER GOD WANTS FOR ME." COMMIT THE LIST TO GOD AND PUT IT IN A SAFE PLACE FOR FUTURE REFERENCE.

PRAYER

I do not know what is next in my life, but God, I trust in Your love and Your promises, and believe in my heart that a bright future awaits me.

SELF-IMAGE

THE TRUE MEASURE OF A PERSON'S WORTH AND BEAUTY IS A MATTER OF THE HEART.

*The value of a person is not measured
on an applause meter; it is measured
in the heart and mind of God.*

JOHN FISCHER

 TO THINK ABOUT

- What are your personal characteristics that you would consider to be your greatest strengths?
- What are some areas of your life where you struggle with self-acceptance?
- How would realizing just how much God loves you help you love yourself and others more?

LESSON FOR LIFE

PROMISES

God will...

Judge you by your faith, not your level of perfection

Galatians 2:16

Accept you

Romans 3:30

Delight in you

Psalm 147:10-11

Precious in His Sight

BIBLE STUDY PASSAGE: EPHESIANS 3:14-21

In Christ we are set free by the blood of his death, and so we have forgiveness of sins. How rich is God's grace, which he has given to us so fully and freely.

EPHESIANS 1:7-8

Why do we find it so hard to share our true self with others? Deep down, a lot of us are afraid that if someone were to truly know us—really get to know us at the core of our being—then there is no possible way that they could love and respect us.

The amazing truth of our Bible study verses is that God, who knows us best, also loves us the very most. The verbs found in Ephesians 1 wonderfully describe God's love for us and are powerful expressions of the intensity of His feelings for us: He chooses us; He lavishes grace on us; He predestines us—even before we were born—to be His children. We also read in this chapter that He redeems us and forgives our sins through the sacrifice of Jesus Christ.

What makes this love even more remarkable is that God doesn't meet our needs with complaining and eye-rolling—*I*

72

created them, I guess I have to save them—but "according to His good pleasure" (v. 9 NKJV). It pleases God to love us. Just as a parent loves her child, so God loves us (v. 12).

But how well does God really know me? Does He really understand how bad and ugly my attitudes and actions have been? Be assured, God knows everything—and He lavishes His love on you with full wisdom and understanding (v. 8).

If the two great needs of being human are to love and to be loved, then you are doubly blessed because of God's love for you. That gives you all the reasons and resources you need to love others—and yourself.

God does not see the same way people see. People look at the outside of a person, but the Lord looks at the heart.

1 Samuel 16:7

God's Mirror

ANALISHA A., AS TOLD TO T. SUZANNE ELLER

From the time I was in first grade, people have called me ugly. When I entered high school, I hoped it would be different. Surely I would be surrounded by people who were more mature and who would accept me. On the first day of school, I overheard a group of people talking. One guy said that if he were as ugly as me, he would kill himself.

So much for a new start.

Nine years. That's a long time to hear people call you names. When I looked in the mirror, I began to see myself as they did. I started to think about suicide and got really depressed. How could God love me if I was this unattractive?

As I grew older and my appearance began to change, the cruel words finally stopped, but I still felt as ugly as ever. I lived as if the taunts and jokes were my identity. I loved God, and I knew that I was a good person. I cared about people. I had many good friends that I loved and who loved me back. God had even assured me in my prayer time that He was with me. I understood all of that, but I couldn't get past the skewed view of myself when I looked into a mirror.

When I turned sixteen, I had to face the hard fact that I had never had a boyfriend, and I decided this meant that all the hurtful words about me were true. Depression began to creep back in. I knew that I didn't want to go back to that dark place, so I took a chance. I talked to my youth pastor and to some good friends about how I felt. They reacted in total surprise. They had no clue that I felt the way I did. My friends helped me to understand that I was looking in the wrong mirror for the answers. I had allowed people who didn't care for me to shape how I saw myself.

For the first time, I took a long look in God's mirror, and there I was—His child, His creation! God made me the way that I am. He delighted in me.

Today I am truly happy. I will never understand why people are cruel or why they say things that are so hurtful. I'm not sure why I faced teasing for such a long time, but I'm not angry. All I'm called to do is love the people who hurt me. In my youth group, I look for people who walk through the door with that look on their face—uncertain, not sure if they will be accepted—and I go to them and welcome them.

Sometimes I feel the thoughts trying to steal back into my mind. When that happens, I push them away by taking a good long look in God's mirror, and I love what I see: His love staring back at me.

ACTION STEP

ON A PIECE OF PAPER, WRITE OUT PSALM 139:13-14: "YOU MADE MY WHOLE BEING; YOU FORMED ME IN MY MOTHER'S BODY. I PRAISE YOU BECAUSE YOU MADE ME IN AN AMAZING AND WONDERFUL WAY." TAPE IT TO YOUR MIRROR AND SAY A PRAYER OF THANKS EVERY TIME YOU READ IT.

BUT DON'T STOP THERE. IF YOU'RE NOT FEELING SO GREAT ABOUT YOURSELF, ONE GREAT WAY TO LIFT YOUR SPIRITS IS TO HELP SOMEONE ELSE WITH THE SAME STRUGGLE. WRITE A NOTE TO A FRIEND WITH THE SAME SCRIPTURE PASSAGE AND A LIST OF THINGS YOU LIKE AND ADMIRE ABOUT THAT PERSON. OR USE A DRY-ERASE MARKER TO WRITE ENCOURAGING WORDS ON A SIBLING'S MIRROR. REMEMBER THAT ALL OF US FEEL INSECURE FROM TIME TO TIME.

PRAYER

As my Creator, You knew me before I was even born. You know everything about me—my weaknesses as well as my strengths. Thank You for loving me as I am.

SERVING GOD

ONE OF THE GREATEST SOURCES OF PERSONAL JOY IS WHEN WE REACH OUT TO OTHERS IN LOVE AND SERVICE

The most infectiously joyous men and women
are those who forget themselves in thinking
about others and serving others.

ROBERT J. MCCRACKEN

 TO THINK ABOUT

- Who are people who have modeled a lifestyle of service for you?
- In what ways are you serving others today?
- What gets in the way of servanthood for you?

LESSON FOR LIFE

PROMISES

God will...

Bless you as you help

others

Psalm 41:1

Allow you to serve Him

freely and with joy

Romans 7:6

Lift up those who serve

Mark 10:43-44

Give you things to do for

Him

Ephesians 2:10

The Towel and Basin Society

BIBLE STUDY PASSAGE: JOHN 13:1-20

If I, your Lord and Teacher, have washed your feet, you also should wash each other's feet. I did this as an example so that you should do as I have done for you.

JOHN 13:14-15

Jesus' disciples seemed to wonder a lot about who was His favorite.   In fact, two of the disciples, James and John, asked their mother to help them get the seats of honor in Jesus' kingdom.   She asked Him: "Promise that one of my sons will sit at your right side and the other will sit at your left side in your kingdom" (Matthew 20:21).

Jesus' response was that she didn't know what she was asking.   She and her sons were interested in the frills and benefits of power, but not the sacrifice involved.   Otherwise, these sons of Zebedee could have been on Jesus' left and right when he prayed in the Garden (Matthew 26:40-46).   Instead, they slept.

They could have been on His left and right when He was arrested (Mark 14:50).   Instead, they fled.

They could have been on His left and right when He hung on a cross (Matthew 15:27, Luke 23:49, John 19:16-19, 26). Instead, they stayed quietly in the crowd.

When Jesus taught His disciples the true meaning of greatness, He taught with a towel and basin. He washed their feet—the duty of a house servant. Peter, still unable to comprehend the object lesson, initially refused to let Jesus lower himself in such a way.

We live in a competitive, "me-first" world. Examples of humility, kindness, helpfulness, and caring for others first—servanthood—are hard to find. A lot of people are just out for themselves.

But the truth is that the happiest and most fulfilled people are those who follow Jesus as members of the "Towel and Basin Society."

Praise the Lord! Happy are those who respect the Lord, who want what he commands.

Psalm 112:1

REAL LIFE

Boomerang Blessings

AMBER EGELSTON AS TOLD TO ESTHER M. BAILEY

Our youth group had a short-term mission trip coming up, and we needed to raise money—quickly. Fortunately, our youth pastor came up with a new twist to the usual fundraisers. He put a bright-colored flyer in the church bulletin that read RENT-A-KID. Our names were listed with phone numbers and services offered.

I was open to just about any kind of work, but I listed babysitting, housework, and cooking. As I sat by the phone and wondered what results I might get, I received a call. "Amber, I don't have any jobs for you, but I do have a proposal. If I give you a check for a hundred dollars, would you like to work it out by doing good deeds for people who can't afford to pay?"

Cool, I thought as ideas already began forming in my mind. "I'll get started on that right away," I said.

When I asked how much work I should do, my sponsor said, "I'll leave that entirely up to you."

Through contacts in my church, I knew about a family that really needed help. The husband was paralyzed from the waist down and was in poor general health. His wife worked outside the home in addition to caring for her husband and their three children. On three occasions, I volunteered my services to watch the kids and tidy up the house.

One time, I worked for eleven hours straight. The job was quite challenging at times, especially when the kids got really wild. Some of those hours seemed to crawl! Each time I finished the task, though, I felt fulfilled and deeply content. Their expressions of appreciation really touched my heart and made me feel good about myself.

By this time I figured I had earned the hundred dollars, but I wanted to go the extra mile.

With several of my friends, I spent a Saturday morning painting over graffiti on the walls of a local residential area. I didn't find the job taxing at all. The families were so grateful for our help that it made the work almost fun.

After I returned from the mission trip to Mexico, the desire to do community service was in my blood. Through the Christian school I attend, I volunteered to help plan a party for impoverished children. Watching the joy on the children's faces and their excitement over the littlest things made all the preparations worthwhile.

When my school planned a service trip to a poor church in Mexico, I volunteered to go along. We conducted church services, prepared meals, chopped firewood, and painted a building. Fellowship with the other students and the congregational members more than made up for any sacrifice I made. It truly amazed me to see how happy they are with so little.

All of these experiences and others have helped me make a commitment to expand my time in service to the community. I truly enjoy helping people, but it seems I get the best deal. The blessings I hope to bring to others always bounce back to me.

ACTION STEP

DO YOU KNOW A FAMILY WHO COULD USE SOME FREE BABYSITTING, OR A PARK THAT NEEDS CLEANING? MAKE ARRANGEMENTS TO HELP SOMEONE THIS SATURDAY—AND DO YOUR BEST TO KEEP YOUR ACT OF SERVICE BETWEEN YOU AND THE PERSON YOU'RE SERVING.

PRAYER

Thank You, God, for sending Jesus into my life and heart with the gift of salvation. Help me to honor that gift through service to others.

OVERCOMING THE PAST

GOD DOES NOT WANT US TO CARRY A LOAD OF GUILT ON OUR BACKS FOREVER, BUT TO ACCEPT HIS FORGIVENESS AND MOVE ON.

If you have behaved badly, repent, make what amends you can and address yourself to the task of behaving better next time. On no account brood over your wrongdoing. Rolling in the muck is not the best way of getting clean.

ALDOUS HUXLEY

 TO THINK ABOUT

- ☛ Is there an old sin that you struggle to let go of and carry with you today?
- ☛ How does not forgiving ourselves thwart God's plans for our lives?
- ☛ Is there someone in your life you need to forgive so they can move on?

LESSON FOR LIFE

PROMISES

God will...

Forgive you

Isaiah 1:18

Cleanse you

1 John 1:9

Work all things for your good

Romans 8:28

Give you freedom

Romans 6:6, 18

God's Amazing Mercy

BIBLE STUDY PASSAGE: PSALM 51

God, be merciful to me because you are loving.   Because you are always ready to be merciful, wipe out all my wrongs.   Wash away all my guilt and make me clean again.

PSALM 51:1-2

You don't understand some of the things I've done.   I'm not sure God can—or would even want to—forgive me.   I've hurt my parents, my teachers, my friends, and myself.

If you've ever messed up, you are not alone.   Even the great heroes of the Bible had serious character flaws and were in need of God's mercy!

Jacob, the son of Isaac and one of the fathers of our faith, tricked his twin brother and even his beloved father, in order to "steal" the family birthright (Genesis 25-27).

Moses, who led the Hebrew slaves from the Pharaoh's oppression in Egypt, murdered a man and lived as a fugitive for forty years (Exodus 2-3).

David, perhaps the most loved and popular king in Israel's

history, performed many acts of courage, faith, and mercy—slaying the giant, Goliath, and sparing King Saul, a sworn enemy to him, to name just two.   But he also had quite a rap sheet.   His greatest crime was what he did to Uriah the Hittite, one of his bravest and most loyal soldiers.   David coveted and then "took" Uriah's wife, Bathsheba.   To make his evil act even worse, he had Uriah killed to try and cover up what he had done.   (See 2 Samuel 11-12 for the whole story.)

Throughout the Psalms, and especially in Psalm 51, David cries for God's mercy.   He knows that being the king doesn't get him off the hook.   He knows that "I'm sorry" can't undo his evil deeds.

There is no sin so great that God's grace is not greater.   Be assured that God's mercy can and will enter a darkened heart and make it pure again.

You will have mercy on us again; you will conquer our sins.   You will throw away all our sins into the deepest part of the sea.
Micah 7:19

REAL LIFE

When I Was a Prodigal Son

DON HALL AS TOLD TO NANETTE THORSEN-SNIPES

It was two days after Thanksgiving when everything went wrong. Clouds pregnant with rain were slung low across the sky that cold day. Mom and my stepdad, Jim, had gone to the store. Before they got home, the phone rang.

"Your father hanged himself." It felt as though someone struck me in the gut.

"Is he dead?" I couldn't cry, but the pain left an empty hole in me—I'd never known him. When the woman said, "Yes," I sat down hard.

A flood of memories came back—my mother threatened by my dad at gunpoint. After he left for work, she moved us out in a hurry. My brother was seven and I was only four.

Maybe that's one reason why I was angry—because my father tried to hurt Mom. I was also angry because he died before I got to know him.

Nothing ever went right for me after that. I couldn't concentrate or learn, and I quit school in the tenth grade. Some days I made life miserable for my parents by drinking and putting my fists through the walls.

One night, I took an unloaded gun from my parents' closet, drove to the hotel where my brother worked, and went straight to the bar.

Inside, a strong, thick-necked man said, "Son, I need to see your ID." Because I didn't have one, I tried to muscle past him. He shoved me. I shoved back. The next thing I knew he smacked me. I pulled the gun, waving it at him.

Meanwhile, someone called the police.

"Freeze!" I turned to see three policemen in a firing stance, their guns aimed at me. They shouted, "Drop your weapon! Get your hands on the wall!" I stood frozen. An inner voice I knew was God prompted me to go to the wall, and I was handcuffed.

So for the umpteenth time, I sat in the county jail. I didn't worry, because Mom would get me out. I was shocked when she refused.

How could I know they'd turned me over to God? There was no way out, and I knew I was in trouble. In desperation, I prayed, *God, please help me.*

A few days later, a friend posted bail. Angrily, I went home, packed, and raced out of the driveway.

Within a year away from my family, I met a young woman and we married. Not long after, we received the Lord. My life was miraculously changed. Anger gave way to love and kindness. And, of course, I started talking to my mom and stepdad again.

One Christmas, Jim and I drove to the store. I looked at him and asked, "Can you ever forgive me for all the pain I've put you through?"

The man I knew as Dad smiled. "I've already forgiven you." Then he put his arm around me, and I remembered the story of the Prodigal Son, and how our Heavenly Father always welcomes us home, too.

ACTION STEP

IF THERE ARE PAST SINS THAT HAVE HAUNTED YOU—AND YOU HAVE TRULY ASKED GOD'S FORGIVENESS—THEN IT IS TIME TO MOVE ON. MAYBE A SYMBOLIC ACT WILL HELP MAKE FORGIVENESS MORE REAL TO YOU. WRITE DOWN THAT THING—OR THOSE THINGS—ON A SHEET OF PAPER AND PLACE IT IN YOUR FIREPLACE (OR ANOTHER SAFE SPOT). SAY A SHORT PRAYER, AND THEN LIGHT THE PAPER ON FIRE AND LET THAT SYMBOLIZE GOD'S ACT OF SCATTERING YOUR SINS AS FAR AS THE EAST IS FROM THE WEST.

PRAYER

Heavenly Father, thank You for saving my soul, forgiving me of my sins, and giving me a new life in You.

TRUSTING GOD

WHETHER TIMES ARE TOUGH OR EASY, FIRM BELIEF IN A GOOD AND LOVING GOD IS THE ONLY ROAD TO SUCCESSFUL LIVING.

Every evening I turn my worries over to God.
He's going to be up all night anyway.

MARY C. CROWLEY

To Think About

- Do you have confidence that God will take care of you and provide what you need—even when life is difficult?
- When things go your way, do you acknowledge that God is the giver of all good gifts?
- Do you ever wait for hard times to come before you to turn to God for help?

LESSON FOR LIFE

PROMISES

God will...

Take on your burdens

Matthew 11:28-29

1 Peter 5:7

Hear your prayers

Deuteronomy 4:7

Psalm 145:18

Be available to help you

Ephesians 2:18

Daily Dependence

BIBLE STUDY PASSAGE: PSALM 40

Trust the Lord with all your heart, and don't depend on your own understanding. Remember the Lord in all you do, and he will give you success.

PROVERBS 3:5-6

We're always being taught the value of responsibility. And yes, being responsible is a very good thing.   But when our attitude reaches the point where we trust more in ourselves than in God, twin temptations, both that lead to spiritual ship-wreck, suddenly confront us.

One temptation is pride, an unhealthy arrogance that slips (or roars) into our thinking when things are going great in our lives.   We become convinced that we are in control of our own world and responsible for all our success.

The second temptation, hopelessness, works itself into our hearts when we face the difficulties of life that are outside of our control—an illness, a difficult relationship, a parent losing a job.

Daily trusting in God—acknowledging that He is the one

source of all good gifts and success and the only safe refuge when life is difficult—steers us from the twin dangers of pride and despair.

James points out that trials test and prove our faith (James 1:1-3), but we don't have to wait for challenging moments to begin trusting God with our entire life. The good news is that with complete and total trust in Him, He directs our steps in the most fulfilling paths for our lives.

Two sparrows cost only a penny, but not even one of them can die without your Father's knowing it. God even knows how many hairs are on your head. So don't be afraid. You are worth much more than many sparrows.
Matthew 10:29-31

REAL LIFE

A Big Worry and a Trusting Cry

JANET LYNN MITCHELL

I was numb, trying to suppress the feeling of panic that hung over me. I had arrived at the hospital to have torn cartilage removed from my knee—no big deal. But when the doctor examined my knees more closely, he discovered that I had a congenital deformity; my knees and feet didn't line up properly.

His words echoed in my head: "Janet, I'm concerned about your future. I'm worried that severe arthritis will develop. The likelihood of you becoming wheelchair bound is great without surgical intervention."

I had gone from a happy-go-lucky teenager to one with an unbelievable worry in a matter of moments. Yet, even with Dr. Allgood's little "discovery," my morning surgery went as planned. Weeks soon passed and I ditched my crutches, but my life seemed to revolve around second, third, and fourth opinions regarding my congenital deformity.

With Dr. Allgood's encouragement, I went to winter camp—skiing with the youth group from my church. From the top of the slope, I scanned the view and realized that my worries had traveled with me. I couldn't imagine being crippled and never walking again. Giving myself a pep talk, my thoughts began to shout. *Janet, you can do this. If having surgery is what I need, I'll have it!*

Despite my determination that I could handle my problems, at the bottom of the run, I found myself worrying again. That night in bed, I hid my face in my pillow as the concerns of my future overwhelmed me. I had done my best to convince my friends that I was fine, but I was scared, fearful of both the known and unknown.

The following night at camp I sat and listened to the speaker. "Don't you think God is big enough to take care of your worries?" he asked. "Do you know how good it feels to let go—to let God do your worrying? Tonight fall back into God's arms and experience Him catching you."

Immediately I began to cry. I could feel my heart pound as I yelled through my thoughts, *No, No, I don't know if I can do this!* I fled the meeting and headed straight to a rustic prayer chapel hidden at the end of a trail. Making sure I was alone, I slipped through the door and knelt below the stained glass window.

God, I'm scared. My worries are too big for me. I need Your help! I want You to do all the worrying that needs to be done. Tears of release streamed from my eyes. Now, for the first time I understood what it meant to have a "trusting cry." In these few moments I told God that I resigned from worrying and fell into His arms. With expectation and trust, I would watch and experience God as He tended to my every need.

ACTION STEP

READ THROUGH HEBREWS 11 IN YOUR NEW TESTAMENT, WHICH PROVIDES A LIST OF OLD TESTAMENT CHARACTERS WHO COMPLETELY TRUSTED GOD— AGAINST ALL ODDS. NOW THINK OF THE TWO OR THREE OF THE MOST DIFFI- CULT MOMENTS IN THE LAST FEW YEARS OF YOUR LIFE. DID YOU FACE THOSE TIMES WITH FAITH IN GOD? IF NOT, HOW WOULD FAITH HAVE MADE A POSI- TIVE DIFFERENCE?

PRAYER

Dear God, I give to You every difficulty and fear that I'm facing—along with every success and good thing—and trust You to provide the strength and grace I need to trust You in every area of my life.

DATING

HOW WE INTERACT WITH MEMBERS OF THE OPPOSITE SEX IMPACTS OUR STATE OF MIND NOW—AS WELL AS OUR FUTURE RELATIONSHIPS.

It is better to be hated for what you are than to be loved for something you are not.

ANDRE GIDE

 TO THINK ABOUT

- ☛ How would you characterize most of the dating relationships among your friends?   Positive?   Negative?   Healthy?   Hurtful?
- ☛ What has been your experience with dating so far?
- ☛ What's the most important thing to learn from being with members of the opposite sex?

LESSON FOR LIFE

PROMISES

God will...

Be faithful

Psalm 118:8

Bless those who trust

Him

Psalm 94:19

Be with you

Hebrews 13:5

Demonstrate true love

1 John 4:9

An Opportunity to Grow

BIBLE STUDY PASSAGE: GENESIS 24:10-67

Even much water cannot put out the flame of love; floods cannot drown love.   If a man offered everything in his house for love, people would totally reject it.

SONG OF SOLOMON 8:7

Dating can be a wonderful opportunity to interact with the opposite sex. We can learn to communicate better; we can experience careful and appropriate levels of affection; we can discover the characteristics we would like to find in a marriage partner and develop these characteristics in ourselves.

Dating can be a horrible way to interact with the opposite sex. We can get caught up in a possessive and jealous relationship; we can lose our innocence by becoming too physical; we can obsess about the opposite sex and lose out on friendships and activities.

Before you begin dating someone, consider the following—

- *You are not abnormal or weird for choosing to wait to date. You have the rest of your life to be with someone. In Ecclesiastes 3:1, Solomon said: "There is a time for everything, and every-*

96

thing on earth has its special season."

- *Your best preparation for a future relationship is how you communicate with members of the opposite sex now. If your dating patterns are not based on positive models of communication—listening, sharing, mutual encouragement, problem solving—you are better off just being friends. "Do not stir up nor awaken love until it pleases" (Song of Solomon 8:4 NKJV).*
- *We need to honor God with all of ourselves, including our relationships. One of the most important elements of any relationship is respecting and valuing what is important to that person. If the person you want to date doesn't value your relationship with God, that's a pretty good indicator that the relationship is not going to honor God or help you grow closer to Him. "You are not the same as those who do not believe. So do not join yourselves to them" (2 Corinthians 6:14).*
- *Don't forget your parents. Even though your parents are asking you to make more and more of your own decisions, don't leave them out of what you're thinking and feeling. Ask them questions. "Honor your father and your mother" (Exodus 20:12).*

God has a wonderful plan for your life. Don't try to rush it when you feel the surge of emotions from someone you are attracted to. The right person will appear to you—at the right time.

Trust the Lord with all your heart, and don't depend on your own understanding. Remember the Lord in all you do, and he will give you success.

Proverbs 3:5-6

97

REAL LIFE

Lessons from a Breakup

NANCY C. ANDERSON

I paced the floor and glared at the clock in the high school cafeteria. My boyfriend, Jason, was supposed to meet me for lunch, but he was late, as usual. So, I went looking for him and walked around the corner near the science lab. There he was, walking hand in hand—with my best friend, Jill!

She had the decency to look away in shame, but he looked me in the eye, smiled a cruel smile, and casually said, "Hi, Nance." They just kept walking. I fell against the wall as my knees and heart folded.

I went through the rest of my classes with a steeled determination not to cry. I made it all the way home. As I locked the door to my bedroom, I unlocked the door to my heart and jagged tears bit my face. I cried until I was empty.

Jason had been my whole world. He was one of most popular boys at school and, when I was with him, I felt important. I liked being defined as "Jason's girlfriend," partly because I hadn't developed any other definition.

I thought, *How could he betray me so easily?*

I tried to pray, but I couldn't get my mouth to form any words. I picked up the Bible by my nightstand and held it to my chest. I whispered, "Help me, Lord." I felt better. Stronger. I opened the book and read the verse in Hebrews 13:5, "God has said, 'I will never leave you; I will never forget you.'"

Then I thought of the song we often sang at church, "On Christ the solid rock I stand, all other ground is sinking sand." I had been standing on Jason and he had crumbled.

During the next few months, I started to rebuild my life and develop my own identity. I auditioned for a part in a play and was thrilled to get a small part. I didn't have any lines, but I was happy just to be part of the team and make new friends. I started to discover things about myself, hidden treasures. I took a creative writing class and poured myself into it. I also volunteered to teach a children's Bible study, got involved in my church's youth group, and took a part-time job at a restaurant.

That winter, I learned a valuable lesson as I watched Jason betray Jill and move on to his next victim.

I never again measured my worth by another person's loyalty to me. As I learned to stand on God's love, and use the gifts He gave me, I saw that He was consistent and unfailing. I also learned that people will disappoint me and I will disappoint myself, but the Lord will never leave me or betray me.

ACTION STEP

HERE ARE FIVE QUESTIONS YOU CAN USE TO EVALUATE YOUR DATING RELATIONSHIPS—OR WHETHER YOU ARE READY FOR A DATING RELATIONSHIP!

- WHAT IS MY MOTIVATION FOR DATING?
- IS THE PERSON I AM DATING A CHRISTIAN?
- DOES MY DATING LIFE INCLUDE SEXUAL IMPURITY?
- AM I A POSITIVE IMPACT ON THE PERSON I'M DATING? ARE THEY A POSITIVE IMPACT ON ME?
- DOES MY DATING RELATIONSHIP PLEASE GOD?

PRAYER

Father God, I know You want what's best for me. Please guide all my decisions and relationships—and help me become the kind of person who has a positive impact on others. Amen.

RECONCILIATION

WITH GOD'S GRACE, EVEN THE MOST DAMAGED RELATIONSHIPS CAN BE RESTORED.

*In some families, please is described
as the magic word. In our house,
however, it was sorry.*

MARGARET LAURENCE

TO THINK ABOUT

- ⚷ Have you experienced the pain of a strained family relationship?
- ⚷ What is the hardest part of healing a broken relationship?
- ⚷ Are there some relationships that get so damaged that they can never be restored?

LESSON FOR LIFE

PROMISES

God will...

Forgive you gladly
Psalm 86:5
1 John 1:9

Help you love others
1 Thessalonians 3:12

Produce patience in you
Galatians 5:22

Messengers of Peace

BIBLE STUDY PASSAGE: EPHESIANS 2:14-22

May the Lord make your love grow more and multiply for each other and for all people so that you will love others as we love you.

1 THESSALONIANS 3:12

Jesus tells His disciples: "If you forgive anyone his sins, they are forgiven. In the Lord's Prayer, He teaches us: "Forgive us for our sins, just as we have forgiven those who sinned against us" (Matthew 6:12).

One of the most important "soul matters" in God's eyes is reconciliation. Just as He sent His Son Jesus into the world to reconcile people to Him (Colossians 1:20-22), so He gives us the mandate to be peacemakers, to be reconciled even to our enemies (Matthew 5:44).

But you don't know how that friend betrayed me. My brother doesn't care about me at all. My sister always knifes me in the back.

Obviously, one person can't do all the work when it comes to making peace. That's why we are told to keep peace "as much as depends on you" (Romans 12:18 NKJV). But before ignoring the call to reconciliation as too hard, too painful, and completely unrealistic, we need to remember—

- *Reconciliation is God's idea and His way of doing things (Romans 5:8-10).*
- *Reconciliation is tied to our relationship with God—He wants us to come before Him with right relationships (Matthew 5:23).*
- *As we forgive others, God forgives us (Luke 6:37).*
- *One of the blessings of walking with God is peace (Galatians 5:22).*

A few notes of caution on this topic include—

- *Reconciliation does not always happen all at once, but can take place over years, so don't give up when you don't see results right away (Galatians 6:9).*
- *Reconciliation does not mean we let others abuse us. Even Jesus told His disciples to "shake the dust from your feet" and avoid certain people (Matthew 10:14).*
- *Even when forgiveness is given both ways, sometimes we can't make a relationship exactly the way it used to be. Someone who has left a spouse and family may seek forgiveness, but not necessarily be able to reenter the lives of those whom they left in the same way.*

Who can you draw close to today? A parent? A friend? A teacher?

Get along with each other, and forgive each other. If someone does wrong to you, forgive that person because the Lord forgave you.
Colossians 3:13

REAL LIFE

The Retreat

ELLEN DUBOIS

My parents were both organists and choir directors at the church in our small town.   Many times, I'd lie to them, saying I'd gone to church when, in fact, I'd simply grabbed a bulletin from the back to bring home as my "proof."

One day, while skipping church as my father was inside playing, I sat in his car with my girlfriend and smoked cigarettes, not thinking that he'd ever see us.

But he did see us. In between songs, he sometimes stepped out into the rear entrance of the church and looked out the window.   Right outside that window was where he parked his car.   I can't imagine his heartache—seeing me, far too young to smoke, skipping church and lying about it.

He never yelled. He simply talked to me in private later that day and reminded me of the little "breaks" he often took while playing.   That was all he had to say.   The look in his eyes was punishment enough.

Around that time, a retreat was planned for the teen members of the church.   I signed up enthusiastically.

So did my younger sister.   We loved each other, but being less than two years apart, we often bickered and argued.   She was a slob, according to me, and I was a bossy know-it-all, according to her.   Even our shared bedroom had an invisible "line" down the middle.

On the second day of the retreat, one of our exercises was to tell someone how much we really loved them and why. My sister and I were paired up. As we stood in God's beautiful forest my sister and I joined hands and shared a moment of silence.

Suddenly, the fights seemed petty. Looking into her eyes, the words slowly formed—"I love you. You are special to me." My heart filled with warmth and I know now that I felt the Holy Spirit working inside of me. She spoke the same words to me and we found ourselves in an embrace of love, tears streaming down both our faces.

What an incredible feeling. I realized that she was a gift from God—in fact, my whole family was a gift. My entire perspective changed in an instant.

In the early evening, as the sun set and the skies above filled with twilight, small campfires were lit. All of us were given candles and were to sit in silence—reflecting.

For the first time, I felt naked and fearful in front of God. I now understood that He was part of me and knew of my lies, my shortcomings, my selfishness—yet He loved me anyway.

I've made my share of mistakes since the retreat. I've relapsed into selfishness with my family. But, by the grace of God I know I am forgiven, and I try with every passing day to be the person that God wants me to be.

ACTION STEP

WHO IS SOMEONE WITH WHOM YOUR RELATIONSHIP IS STRAINED OR BROKEN? HOW SERIOUS IS THE CAUSE OF THE SEPARATION? WHAT MAKES IT HARDEST FOR YOU TO SEEK FORGIVENESS AND RESTORATION? WHAT IS ONE SMALL STEP YOU CAN TAKE TODAY? ARE YOU READY?

PRAYER

Thank You, God, that when I was far away from You and lost, You ventured to seek me out. Grant me the courage to be a peacemaker in my world.

OVERCOMING SELFISHNESS

WE WILL NEVER BE HAPPY AND FULFILLED JUST LOOKING OUT FOR OUR INTERESTS—WE NEED TO REACH OUT AND SHARE WITH OTHERS.

*I've learned that you shouldn't go through life
with a catcher's mitt on both hands.
You need to be able to throw something back.*

AUTHOR UNKNOWN

 TO THINK ABOUT

- Do you find it easier to give or to receive?
- What gets in the way of you helping others?   Do you look for needs in the lives of those around you?
- When have you blessed someone else with your generosity and kindness?

LESSON FOR LIFE

The Way Love Grows

BIBLE STUDY PASSAGE: GALATIANS 6:1-10

We must not become tired of doing good. We will receive our harvest of eternal life at the right time if we do not give up.

GALATIANS 6:9

In the sixth chapter of Galatians, Paul sets out some of the most practical principles for expressing love to others found anywhere in the Bible.   But just because they're practical doesn't mean they're easy!

First, he tells us that we should be redemptive people, helping restore those who have been caught in a sin (v. 1). He does caution you that as you reach out to help someone, be extra careful not to get trapped in sin yourself.

Second, Paul challenges us to love others unconditionally, without judgment and comparisons (v. 4).   Competition can be friendly and healthy, but when it consumes our relationships, the inevitable result is conflict.   How many friendships and sibling relationships have been torpedoed by a spirit of striving rather than a spirit of pulling together?

Next, Paul urges us to help carry the "excessive weights" that others are forced to bear (v. 2). He does point out that each of us should carry our own "backpacks," so we aren't required to do everything for others (v. 5). But when someone has burdens that are bigger than any one person should handle alone, we are to step in help.

Most importantly, Paul reminds us not to give up on loving others (v. 9). Sure, some people are unbelievably difficult to love, but if we don't lose faith in God's power to authentically change their lives, our steadfast persistence may be the very thing that makes the difference between them finding God's forgiveness and peace or never receiving God's grace in their hearts.

The result of how we relate to others is simple, according to Paul. He says, "People harvest only what they plant" (v. 7). When we sow love into others, we will ultimately receive love in return.

Do you know where your fights and arguments come from? They come from the selfish desires that war within you.
James 4:1

REAL LIFE

Strangers in My House

JAMIE C. AS TOLD TO T. SUZANNE ELLER

I stared out the front window, sick to my stomach as I watched the kids climb out of the car and walk to the door. I didn't want to talk to them, but my mom ushered me in front of them and introduced us. The lady from DHS stood in the background, watching to see how the foster kids would react to their new home.

The kids seemed willing to adapt, but I started to put up walls right then and there. I didn't want to have anything to do with these strangers in my house.

I was shocked when my parents decided to open our home to foster kids. The thought of them moving in and rearranging our lives did not sound pleasant. I felt like my parents were trying to replace me, like God had turned His back on me.

When the foster kids arrived, I did everything I could to annoy them. I looked for opportunities to show my parents why this was a bad decision. I prayed every night that God would take these people out of my home and return everything back to normal.

One night, I was praying my same old prayers when He shared something with me: If these kids didn't live with us, they might never have the chance to know who He is or that He loves them. I sat on my bed as God made me face the truth—the kids that came to our home might never understand what it means to be secure.

I let the walls crumble that night. I asked God to forgive me. After that, it wasn't fun picking on my foster brothers and sisters anymore.

One day I had the perfect opportunity to be kind. My foster sister had messed up, and if I told my parents, she would be in big trouble. I had compassion for her and kept my mouth shut.

Some of my foster brothers and sisters have been hurt so much that they don't know how to trust. Some have been neglected and feel abandoned. I can't solve those problems, but I can share with them that God loves them and hasn't turned His back on them. In fact, He brought them to our home so He could give them a dose of His love.

After two years of living with the kids, I'm not the same old Jamie. I accept life as it comes. I'm thankful for the love my parents have for me—and for others. I'm more open and compassionate toward people and the problems they face.

Our family is not perfect. Sometimes my siblings and I fight, just like everyone else, and we all have to adjust when a new kid comes. But there is one major difference: When I see the stranger walking to the door, I'm there to welcome my new foster brother or sister to their new home.

ACTION STEP

LOOK FOR A SPECIAL NEED AT YOUR SCHOOL, IN YOUR NEIGHBORHOOD, OR IN YOUR CHURCH. ASK GOD TO IMPRESS ON YOUR HEART WHAT YOU CAN GIVE TO BLESS THAT PERSON OR FAMILY IN THEIR SITUATION. IF AT ALL POSSIBLE, MAKE YOUR GIFT IN SECRET AND KEEP IT BETWEEN YOU AND GOD.

PRAYER

Lord God, You bless me in so many ways. Help me bless others the way You have blessed me—help me see others with Your eyes.

DOING WHAT'S RIGHT

THOUGH IT'S SOMETIMES DIFFICULT, WE PLEASE GOD AND LIVE THE LIFE HE INTENDED FOR US WHEN WE CHOOSE TO FAITHFULLY OBEY HIM.

Whether you know it or not, you're being watched. And the things you model—by design or by accident—powerfully communicate your convictions about right and wrong, about morality and immorality. If you want to pass on values to others, you must model those values in your own life. You must believe them yourself.

JOSH MCDOWELL

TO THINK ABOUT

- Have you ever struggled with obedience in a particular area because it seemed too hard and didn't make perfect sense?
- What are the benefits of obeying God and doing the right thing?
- Is there an area of your life where you don't want to obey right now? What will you do about it?

LESSON FOR LIFE

PROMISES

God will...

Accept you
Romans 15:17

Protect you
Psalm 37:28

Defend you
Psalm 7:10

Bless you
Psalm 1:1

The Obedience of Mary

BIBLE STUDY PASSAGE: LUKE 1:26-56

Mary said, "I am the servant of the Lord. Let this happen to me as you say!"

LUKE 1:38

Mary, the mother of Jesus, is perhaps the best known of all the women of the Bible—people across the world know who she was and honor her. It was to Mary that God first revealed His specific plan to "save his people from their sins" through her Son (Matthew 1:21).

Mary was an ordinary young woman, engaged to a carpenter named Joseph, until one day, an angel suddenly appeared and said, "Greetings! The Lord has blessed you and is with you" (Luke 1:28), changing her life forever. The angel told her that she had been chosen to carry Jesus, the Savior of the world.

Mary could have asked a lot of questions—"What will Joseph think?" "What will happen to us?" If Mary was thinking these questions, she didn't say so. She never argued or said, "Let me think this over." She simply said yes to God's

114

plan: "Let this happen to me as you say" (Luke 1:38).   She placed her reputation, her marriage, and her entire life at risk to be obedient to God—and trusted that His will was perfect.

And because of her trust and obedience, salvation became available to all humanity.

Mary's simple faith and readiness to do God's will brought the blessing of God into her life—and that same faith and obedience will bless your life today.

Those who make evil plans will be ruined, but those who plan to do good will be loved and trusted.

Proverbs 14:22

REAL LIFE

Just a Typical Teenage Boy

STACI STALLINGS

The call was controversial—just as all really close calls in baseball are. The runner slid home full speed, and stood up expecting loud cheers for scoring the winning run, only to hear the umpire yell, "You're out!"

Furious, he threw off his helmet and ran over to explain to the ump in no uncertain terms why the call was wrong, why the ump needed glasses, and why he was clearly home and nobody could miss that call so badly. Before his temper really got out of hand, someone pulled him away, and he walked to the bench—livid.

Long after the coaches, players, and fans had gone home, the high schooler realized the impact of the decisions he'd made back at home plate. Like most of us do when we are faced with the embarrassment of our actions, he could very well have just let it slide, reasoning: "Everybody does it. The ump's probably heard that stuff a million times."

However, in the silence of his heart, this young man knew that just because everyone else does it, that doesn't make it right. And so, long after his buddies had gone home, he went back to the school to find the umpire—not to vandalize his car or further harangue him, but to tell him face-to-face, "I'm sorry, sir. I was wrong."

When he found him, he gave a true apology—one not meant for the world to hear or to make the apologizer look better in the eyes of anyone else. It was meant simply as a way to stay true to what his heart was telling him.

On the way out of town, the umpire saw the superintendent and flagged him down to express his appreciation and surprise at the boy's apology. But the ump wasn't the only one who was surprised. The superintendent later talked to the coach to say how impressed he was that the coach had sent the boy to apologize—only the coach hadn't sent him and knew nothing about the apology until that very moment.

A few days later, the coach ran into the boy's father and remarked how impressed he was that his parents had sent the boy to apologize. But the boy's parents knew nothing about it, either.

Although the boy's parents didn't intervene on this occasion, they had intervened enough times in the past for him to have the courage to try to remedy a situation when it would have been easier to reason, "He'll get over it."

Courage is a matter of the heart. I wish that every person in the whole world had the courage of this one student in my youth group. Even though he was the student and I was the leader, he inspired me to do what's right—even when it's difficult.

ACTION STEP

SECOND CHRONICLES 7:14 SAYS "THEN IF MY PEOPLE, WHO ARE CALLED BY MY NAME, ARE SORRY FOR WHAT THEY HAVE DONE, IF THEY PRAY AND OBEY ME AND STOP THEIR EVIL WAYS, I WILL HEAR THEM FROM HEAVEN. I WILL FORGIVE THEIR SIN, AND I WILL HEAL THEIR LAND."

WRITE OUT YOUR OWN PRAYER OF HUMBLE REPENTANCE, ASKING GOD TO FORGIVE AREAS OF DISOBEDIENCE AND HELP YOU MAKE ANY CHANGES IN YOUR LIFE THAT NEED TO BE MADE.

PRAYER

Father God, help me remember that Your will is good, pleasing, and perfect. Thank You so much that You reward those who do what's right. I pray that Your will would be done in my life every day. Help me humbly follow You.

RECEIVING GOD'S LOVE

GOD'S LOVE IS AVAILABLE TO EVERYONE, BUT IT IS UP TO US TO OPEN OUR HEARTS AND RECEIVE IT.

Every one of us as a human being is known and loved by the Creator apart from every other human on earth.

JAMES DOBSON

TO THINK ABOUT

- ☛ Have you ever struggled to accept that others truly love you? That God loves you?
- ☛ Why do some of us resist receiving love and affection?
- ☛ What must you do in your heart to be more open to God's love?

LESSON FOR LIFE

PROMISES

God will...

Never stop loving you

Romans 8:38-39

Pour His love into your heart

Romans 5:5

1 John 4:9-10

Save you by His mercy

Titus 1:4-5

Draw people to himself

Hosea 2:19

A Bigger Heart

BIBLE STUDY PASSAGE: LUKE 19:1-10

The Father has loved us so much that we are called children of God. And we really are his children.

1 JOHN 3:1

If you grew up attending church, maybe you remember singing a song about a small man named Zacchaeus: *Zacchaeus was a wee little man, Oh, a wee little man was he. So he climbed up in a sycamore tree for the Lord he wanted to see.*

We don't know a lot about Zacchaeus' background, but we do know he was a small man—but not just because of his height. Like the Grinch from Dr. Seuss, what was truly small was his heart. A corrupt tax collector, he stole from his own people on behalf of the Romans, and as a result, they despised him and he despised them.

But apparently, deep in his soul, Zacchaeus wanted something more—something bigger—in his life. He didn't want more money. He wanted to love and to be loved. That all became possible when Jesus entered his life.

He opened his home to Jesus—and those he once despised.   Unlike the rich young ruler who loved money more than people, Zacchaeus opened his pocketbook and paid back even more than he had stolen.   Most of all, he opened his heart to the life-changing power of God's love.   And like the Grinch, his heart grew three sizes in an instant.

The question is never whether God loves you.   The real question is whether you will open your heart and receive that love.   Your life, your soul, your heart will grow bigger than they could ever be without Him.

All people will know that you are my followers if you love each other.

John 13:35

 REAL LIFE

New Life

JAMIE LAMOURE AS TOLD TO EILEEN ZYGARLICKE

For five days I sat in a chair. I said nothing. I did nothing. I just sat there, mad that I was in another placement. I hadn't lived at home in two years. Now I was in my first foster home and I hated it.

My foster parents talked to me and treated me like one of their own kids, even when I refused to speak. Very slowly, I started talking again, just a little at first—and soon I was laughing and joking around with them.

Their whole life was different from mine. They ate meals together, something I thought only happened on TV. They also talked, not yelled, when communicating. Life with them was different, but a good kind of different.

Sometimes they would talk to me about God, invite me to church with them, or just tell me how much God loved me. My usual response was to just blow them off. One night, though, my foster dad and I talked about who God was. I didn't know. I used His name often, but not in very flattering terms. When my foster dad told me he prayed for me daily and that God had impressed upon him things about me, I was creeped out. At least until we talked more. Then I saw that those "God things" were pretty accurate. It got me thinking that maybe God did care.

Weeks turned to months, and before long it was time for me to leave. I didn't really want to go—my family was moving to another state, but a big part of me wanted to stay with my fosters. I knew they cared. I knew they loved me. But I also knew we'd keep in touch.

I would call sometimes to let them know how I was doing and to let them talk to my newest boyfriend. They would tease and joke with me about raising the bar in terms of dating—some of my boyfriends had been in jail or were in the process of going to trial. I honestly didn't think much about it at the time, but now I can see why they were concerned.

One day I called with news I didn't think they were expecting to hear. I was dating someone new. I had raised my standards and stopped dating the criminal element. I had met this boyfriend at work. We started talking, and before I knew it, I was sitting in a youth group next to him. I was actually in church! Not only was I in church, but this whole God stuff was finally starting to make sense. I made a decision in that church to begin to live my life for Jesus. And once I made that decision, I knew who I needed to call.

My foster parents cheered when I told them the news of my decision. "Now you're eternally part of our family," my foster mom said. And you know what? Nothing could make me happier.

ACTION STEP

"I HOPE YOU DANCE" IS A FAMOUS SONG FROM SEVERAL YEARS AGO BY LEE ANN WOMACK. ONE OF THE LINES IS: "AND WHEN YOU GET THE CHOICE TO SIT IT OUT OR DANCE, I HOPE YOU DANCE."

DO YOU SAY YES TO GOD'S LOVE AND THE OPPORTUNITIES HE PLACES IN YOUR LIFE? WHAT IS ONE OPPORTUNITY YOU'VE SAID "NO" TO RECENTLY? IS THERE SOMETHING YOU SHOULD ACTUALLY BE DOING? IT'S NOT TOO LATE TO REVERSE COURSE. ASK GOD TO HELP YOU BE A "YES" PERSON.

PRAYER

Dear Heavenly Father, thank You so much for Your love. God, please come and heal and fill my heart today.

GIVING

GOD BLESSES US AND CALLS US TO SHARE OUR BLESSINGS WITH THOSE IN NEED.

*To give and then not feel that one has given
is the very best of all ways of giving.*

MAX BEERBOHM

TO THINK ABOUT

- 🔑 When have you been blessed by someone's generosity?
- 🔑 When have you blessed someone else with your generosity?
- 🔑 Do you find it easier to give or to receive?

LESSON FOR LIFE

The Gift of Giving

BIBLE STUDY PASSAGE: ROMANS 12:1-10

"Bring to the storehouse a full tenth of what you earn so there will be food in my house.   Test me in this," says the Lord All-Powerful.   "I will open the windows of heaven for you and pour out all the blessings you need."

MALACHI 3:10

One of the true tests of our character is what we do with our money. Of course, God calls us to give a portion of our income to Him through ministry (Numbers 18:28) and to also give special sacrificial offerings to meet special needs as we feel directed in our hearts (Numbers 15:3). Paul does say that some people have a special gift of giving (Romans 12:8), but he also points out that God loves a cheerful giver (2 Corinthians 9:7), and Jesus himself drew attention to the small gift of a poor widow as a true model of generosity (Matthew 12:43-44).

When we are generous, a number of healthy dynamics—

• *We acknowledge that God owns everything and we have only been appointed as caretakers. The psalmist declares on behalf*

126

of God: *"Every animal of the forest is already mine. The cattle on a thousand hills are mine" (Psalm 50:10).*

- We clutch less tightly to what we can earn and hoard and become more aware that all good gifts come from God. James tells us: *"Every perfect gift is from God" (James 1:17).*

- We learn to trust and serve God with a pure heart. Jesus told His disciples: *"No one can serve two masters. The person will hate one master and love the other, or will follow one master and refuse to follow the other. You cannot serve both God and worldly riches" (Matthew 6:24).*

- We receive the joy that comes from helping someone in need *(Matthew 25:23).*

- We become more confident and trusting, and begin to eliminate worry from our lives *(Philippians 4:5-7, 17).*

- We become better stewards in all areas of our finances; there is a strange paradox that the more we give, the more we seem to have *(Matthew 19:29).*

> Whoever gives to others will get richer; those who help others will themselves be helped.
>
> Proverbs 11:25

The most important gift that God wants you to offer Him is your very life (Romans 12:1-2). Then He can teach you that whatever we selfishly grasp dries up in our hands. Whatever we give freely takes off and soars.

REAL LIFE

The Best Summer Job Ever

My friend Chris and I took our smiling pictures on a digital camera. We then added them to a flyer we were making to advertise our lawn mowing service. The going rate in our area for cutting, edging, sweeping, and bagging was about $35. Since we still needed a little practice on the edging—and we were both only fourteen—we offered a great deal of $25 for a normal yard. First cut was a special rate of $15.

We passed out more than 200 flyers, and sure enough, we got 23 responses. Of that number, we ended up with 15 regular customers

For about six months of late spring, summer, and early fall, we cut almost 500 yards. After buying gas and storing our equipment at the end of the summer, we both ended up with almost $5,000.

Our parents were proud. I was very excited about having my own spending money—it was just me and my mom at my house, so we didn't have a lot of extra cash—and a great start on buying a pickup truck in two years. If I saved a good portion of the money from two more seasons of cutting, I'd have a good chunk of change to buy something used, but pretty nice.

I was sitting in church a couple Sundays later and there was a special speaker who was a medical missionary from Papua New Guinea—a country on the other side of the world I'd never heard of before. He talked about the day-to-day needs and hardships among the poor there. Now it was even worse after storms and tidal waves.   Out of nowhere, I felt God tell me to give $1,000 to the offering.   My immediate response was to groan.   No way, I thought.   I worked too hard for that money to just give it away.

But I knew God was telling me to do it.   When I told my mom what was on my heart, she was actually pretty sympathetic to me.   She asked if I was sure I was understanding God correctly.

I was sure.   When I wrote the check and sealed and addressed the envelope, she smiled and squeezed my hand and said she would treat me for some ice cream since my wallet was officially empty again.   We both laughed and I actually meant it.   I felt like I'd done the right thing.

Chris and I already have fifteen customers set for next summer and if we can land a few more, we'll make more money, and I'm sure I'll end up with a great truck.   But I won't forget to thank God for blessing me so much—or to ask Him how He wants to use my money.

ACTION STEP

DO YOU KEEP A BUDGET TO MANAGE YOUR ALLOWANCE OR PAYCHECK OR BABY-SITTING EARNINGS? START ONE TODAY: MAKE A LIST OF YOUR EXPENSES—BE SURE TO INCLUDE GIVING TO GOD—AND SET A REALISTIC AMOUNT OF MONEY FOR EACH CATEGORY. THEN LOOK AT HOW MUCH EXTRA SPENDING MONEY YOU HAVE AND PRAYERFULLY CONSIDER A SPECIAL NEED IN YOUR COMMUNITY YOU'D LIKE TO DONATE TO.

PRAYER

I praise You, O God, who meets all my needs and lavishes me with all kinds of blessings. Thank You for enabling me to be generous with others.

CHOICES

THE CHOICES WE MAKE TODAY TRULY IMPACT THE OPPORTUNITIES WE WILL HAVE TOMORROW.

*Though no one can go back and make a brand new start,
anyone can start from now and make a brand new ending.*

AUTHOR UNKNOWN

TO THINK ABOUT

- ☛ Have you had friends who have consistently hurt themselves by making bad decisions?
- ☛ Where do you turn when you have a tough decision to make?
- ☛ What are some of the most important decisions you will make in the next few years?

LESSON FOR LIFE

PROMISES

God will...

Reward wise decisions
Psalm 37:18

Bless you as you seek to
obey Him
James 1:25

Forgive you if you turn
back to Him
Zechariah 1:3

Give you wisdom to
choose wisely
Isaiah 30:21

Decisions, Decisions

BIBLE STUDY PASSAGE: PROVERBS 3

*If you go the wrong way—to the right or to the left—you
will hear a voice behind you saying, "This is the right way.
You should go this way."*

ISAIAH 30:21

The way you make decisions will determine the kind of life
you lead. Consistently make bad decisions and have a consistently hard life. Make wise decisions and live the life God
planned for you. Here are a few reminders—

- *Ask God for wisdom: "But if any of you needs wisdom, you
  should ask God for it. He is generous and enjoys giving to all
  people, so he will give you wisdom" (James 1:5). We ask God to
  help us with all sorts of problems. Why not ask Him for one of
  the greatest gifts in the world—wisdom? He wants to give this
  to you.*
- *Study God's Word: "Your word is like a lamp for my feet and a
  light for my path" (Psalm 119:105). Literacy rates may be going
  up in our culture, but biblical illiteracy is at epidemic levels.*

132

Stand out from the crowd and read God's Word every day.

- *Talk to God throughout the day: "Pray continually" (1 Thessalonians 5:17). We need alone time to pray in a focused way, but we also need to talk to God as if He was with us in every situation—because He is with us in every situation.*
- *Seek smart peer pressure: "Spend time with the wise and you will become wise, but the friends of fools will suffer" (Proverbs 13:20). Get close to people who live their lives and make the kinds of decisions you want for yourself. Be kind and friendly to everyone. But make sure you interact with wise people every day.*
- *Correct your mistakes: "My dear children, I write this letter to you so you will not sin. But if anyone does sin, we have a helper in the presence of the Father—Jesus Christ, the One who does what is right" (1 John 2:1). If you do make a bad choice, don't compound it by staying the course. Swallow your pride. Apologize. Ask forgiveness. Make an immediate U-turn.*

Happy are those who don't listen to the wicked, who don't go where sinners go, who don't do what evil people do. They love the Lord's teachings, and they think about those teachings day and night.

Psalm 1:1-2

REAL LIFE

Maximum Security

NEELY ARRINGTON

I swallowed the lump in my throat as I read the sign—County Juvenile Detention Center. I never dreamed I'd be in a place like this. I sat for what seemed like forever and stared at the tall fences and razor wire surrounding the prison in front of me. I dreaded the cold, unfriendly air that I knew would greet me at the door when I entered.

My heart pounded rapidly as the iron door slammed shut behind me. The burly guard ordered me to walk down the hall with my hands behind my back. The hall seemed endless. Bang! I jumped and turned my head sharply at the unexpected sound. The noise came from the lockdown cell beside me. A pair of angry eyes glared at me through the tiny window in the cell door. I gasped and grabbed the hand of the girl beside me. We were both terrified.

The guard ordered us to keep walking, but the harsh voice connected to those angry eyes called after me. With a barrage of profanity he told me to get out of "his jail" or he would wring my neck. He began violently punching and kicking the cell door. I don't think I've ever been so scared in my life. What was I doing in jail?

Okay, I wasn't actually a prisoner. But nothing could have prepared me for what I encountered during the prison ministry choir tour. Despite numerous lengthy rehearsals, I had no idea this trip would have such a lasting affect on my life. During this ten-day tour, my youth choir, Mirror Image, performed at many different juvenile detention centers. We were there to "reflect the Son" to inmates with song and dance. Visiting both minimum- and maximum-security prisons provided us with many interesting experiences, both pleasant and unpleasant. Through it all, I knew my main purpose was to share my faith with inmates, who might not ever hear of God's love otherwise.

It broke my heart as I watched what looked like just a small boy fidgeting with his orange jumper during one of our performances. He was sentenced to life in prison for murdering his parents as they slept. Hearing this made me realize that no matter how old someone is, he can still make life-altering choices.

I came home from the tour determined to make wise decisions about who my friends are, the activities I participate in, and my future. So many times I take having a loving home and caring family for granted. After this trip, my home and the relationships I have with my family and friends became even more important to me. Instead of wanting something more or different, I am very grateful for my life just as it is.

ACTION STEP

WHAT ARE THE FIVE BIGGEST DECISIONS YOU HAVE TO MAKE THIS YEAR?
WRITE THEM DOWN. NOW WRITE DOWN THE FIVE BIGGEST DECISIONS YOU
HAVE TO MAKE BEFORE YOU GRADUATE FROM HIGH SCHOOL.

AFTER ASKING GOD TO GIVE YOU THE WISDOM TO MAKE GREAT DECISIONS
TODAY AND THROUGHOUT YOUR TEEN YEARS, TUCK THIS LIST SOMEWHERE
SAFE AND CHECK OUT HOW YOU'RE DOING EVERY THREE MONTHS OR SO.

PRAYER

*Father God, sometimes it scares me to realize how much impact my decisions
have on my life. Thanks for being there to advise me—and thanks that my life
is in Your hands.*

TREATING EVERYONE WITH KINDNESS

WE CHANGE THE WORLD ONE PERSON AT A TIME BY THE WAY WE TREAT EACH PERSON WE MEET.

*Too often we underestimate the power of a touch, a smile,
a kind word, a listening ear, an honest compliment, or the smallest
act of caring, all of which have the potential to turn a life around.*

LEO BUSCAGLIA

TO THINK ABOUT

- ⚷ When was the last time you were surprised by the level of someone's kindness toward you?
- ⚷ How often do you surprise others by your acts of kindness?
- ⚷ How is kindness one of the most pure forms of showing God's love?

LESSON FOR LIFE

PROMISES

God will...

Bless your efforts at
kindness
Romans 12:20

Bless you
1 Peter 3:9
Proverbs 14:21

Reward you for your
kindness
Galatians 6:10

A Good Neighbor

BIBLE STUDY PASSAGE: LUKE 10:25-37

*This is what the Lord All-Powerful says: "Do what is right
and true. Be kind and merciful to each other."*

ZECHARIAH 7:9

Some religious leaders challenged Jesus with a question
about who we should consider our neighbor. In other words,
who was acceptable and who was unacceptable?

Jesus gave them an answer, but not to the question they
asked. Instead of telling them who their neighbor is, He told
them what a good neighbor looks like through the powerful
story of the Good Samaritan.

Note, many Jewish leaders of Jesus' day would have
nothing to do with Samaritans, so you can imagine how mad
they were that Jesus made a Samaritan the hero of the story—
and the model for kindness.

In taking care of a fellow traveler who had been beaten
and robbed, the Samaritan teaches us that—

- Kindness can be costly: "The next day, the Samaritan brought out two coins, gave them to the innkeeper, and said, 'Take care of this man. If you spend more money on him, I will pay it back to you when I come again'" (Luke 10:35). No question, kindness requires effort—and sometimes even sacrifice on our part.
- Kindness can be risky: "Evil people will not learn to do good even if you show them kindness" (Isaiah 26:10). Just as the Samaritan man risked being mugged himself by slowing down to help, at times our kindness will be taken advantage of.
- Kindness turns enemies into friends: "The Samaritan went to him, poured olive oil and wine on his wounds, and bandaged them. Then he put the hurt man on his own donkey and took him to an inn where he cared for him" (Luke 10:34). If this Jew and Samaritan could be united through kindness, what might happen to your relationships as you become a good neighbor?
- Kindness saves people's lives: "A smiling king can give people life; his kindness is like a spring shower" (Proverbs 16:15). There are countless teens at your school who have all but given up on a good God because of how they've been mistreated. You can change their perspective with kindness.

Who can you be a neighbor to today?

Most importantly, love each other deeply, because love will cause many sins to be forgiven.
1 Peter 4:8

REAL LIFE

Billy the Bully

ROBIN BAYNE

"I won't date a guy who fights," I told Jim, the guy with whom I was becoming a little bit more than friends. On occasion, he picked a fight. Once, I'd glimpsed him in a boxing stance and flashed back to my early childhood. I'd been bullied. I can recall in vivid detail walking home from school with a smirking red-haired boy, Billy, walking backward in front of me with his fists in my face.

My parents had discussions with his, but they scoffed, insisting he was just being a boy. Anxiety often gripped my belly during my grade school days. Sooner or later, it was just me and Billy, and he lived directly behind me.

"I used to be pathetic because of a bully," I told Jim now. "It's not something I can deal with in a boyfriend."

"If it's that important to you, I'll work on it."

"Thank you." I gave him a big smile. "Now let's go for a drive where I grew up."

Jim nodded, and I looked from house to house as we drove. As we neared Billy the Bully's house, I saw a cluster of people in the front yard.

"Slow down." I said, then plastered my finger to the window. "That's him!" "Who?"

"Billy, and his parents. They still must live here."

The car slowed and my gaze settled on Billy. I'd recognize that bright hair and freckled face anywhere.   His ears stuck out like handles.   He hadn't changed a bit!

"Should I stop and punch his lights out?"

"No!"

"Just checking.   You want me to tell him off?   You know, he could never get a girl as pretty as you.   That should make you feel good."

My pulse pounded and I felt perspiration trickle down my sides.   But Jim was wrong—I didn't feel good.   In fact, the longer I looked at Billy, the worse I felt.

For him.

Like the Grinch's heart on Christmas morning, mine expanded and I suddenly felt bad for the guy.   I knew better than to judge anyone by their looks alone, but I suddenly hoped Billy would find someone to love him.   We're supposed to treat others as we want to be treated—and I didn't want any "revenge" for the past.

I decided to pray for Billy.

"So what do we do?" Jim asked.

"Let's just go," I said, and glanced at Billy one more time, glad Jim didn't seem bent on punishing him for his grade school crimes.   Billy stood cross-armed, watching us drive away.   He hadn't noticed me or hadn't recognized me.   But it didn't matter.

"I don't think these memories are going to bother me anymore," I said.   It was time to leave my old neighborhood behind and forgive.   I sent up my prayers—for me, and for Billy the Bully

ACTION STEP

A MOVEMENT THAT HAS BEEN QUITE POPULAR IS CALLED RANDOM ACTS OF KINDNESS. THERE WAS EVEN A DAY OF THE YEAR DEDICATED TO GOING ABOVE AND BEYOND IN A LAVISH ACT OF GOODNESS TOWARD OTHERS. THOUGH KINDNESS CAN'T JUST BE FOR A DAY, WE MUST START SOMEWHERE.

PICK A DAY THIS WEEK AND PLOT OUT THREE OR FOUR KIND DEEDS YOU WILL DO FOR FAMILY MEMBERS AND FRIENDS AT SCHOOL. HAVE A LOT OF FUN WITH THIS ACTIVITY!

PRAYER

God, thank You so much for Your kindness to me, and the kindness shown to me by so many people. Help me be an instrument of Your kindness to someone today.

ROLE MODELS

TO REACH OUR FULL POTENTIAL, WE ALL NEED SOMEONE TO LOOK UP TO AND LEARN FROM.

When the student is ready,
the teacher will appear.

CHINESE PROVERB

TO THINK ABOUT

- Is there someone in your life you look up to and want to be like?
- How open are you to guidance and instruction from someone who is older and wiser?
- Are you ready with a little advice and encouragement for those who are younger and less experienced than you are?

LESSON FOR LIFE

PROMISES

God will...

Send people to help you

grow

1 Corinthians 4:17

Reward the faithful

Revelation 2:10

Produce fruit in your life

Galatians 5:22

Speak to you through

others

Luke 1:45

Live and Learn

BIBLE STUDY PASSAGE: 1 TIMOTHY 1:1-10

Follow my example, as I follow the example of Christ.
1 Corinthians 11:1

We don't know much about Paul's student Timothy from his own words, but from Paul's letters to him in the New Testament, we discover he deeply appreciated his godly heritage (1 Timothy 1:5), he carefully followed the teaching of his mentor (1 Timothy 1:19), and as a result, he was wise beyond his years as a minister and leader (1 Timothy 4:12).

If you want to be a great leader, you must be willing to be a great follower—to choose the right role models and learn from them.   An exhausted, ineffective, frustrated Moses could not keep up with the demands of leading his people—until he listened to the counsel of his father-in-law (Exodus 18:24). That takes humility and courage!

Bottom line, we would all do better if we had a trusted mentor in our lives, and that won't happen until our hearts are open and we are humble enough to learn from someone else.

If you want to get better grades, study with a straight-A

student.   If you want to improve your tennis game, play with kids who are better than you.   If you want to grow spiritually, look for a friend or adult who really shows spiritual grace and joy.   And then pass along what you've learned to others!

Keep your eyes focused on what is right, and look straight ahead to what is good.

Proverbs 4:25

REAL LIFE

Steady as Mashed Potatoes

SANDRA RAILSBACK

He had a cleft palate and bug eyes. I never heard him say anything profound, just "Hi Sandy, how're ya doing?" Yet from this simple peanut-butter-and-jelly kind of guy I learned something about faithfulness and giving.

Every Saturday night for four years Dave Thomas showed up at my church to play volleyball and board games, scoop ice cream, and lead prayer. I didn't know it then, but he sacrificed time with his wife and four children to teach us about faithfulness. One such Saturday night Dave drove twenty of us teenagers to sing at a church in a neighboring town. He often drove us places in an old green bus affectionately nicknamed the "tin can," as we sang loud, happy songs while bouncing along the highway. On this particular night, we performed a musical drama called "Celebrate Life."

We had worked hard preparing costumes and memorizing songs and were excited to be part of the service. Dave had watched that drama at least a dozen times and took it as seriously as we did. We were doing something worthy of God's kingdom, and he let us know that. Being able to minister through music and drama changed me forever. I didn't pursue a career in music ministry—I can barely keep up with an easy hymn during worship—but working with Dave and the other students instilled in me the idea that I can minister in my own way.

On our way home, we stopped at a Denny's. A few of the teenage boys began poking fun at a shy girl. Dave made them stop. He simply said, "Hey, guys, that's enough." Never did he raise his voice; never did he call attention to the shy girl. The boys just stopped. Dave, with his slight frame and balding head, had our deep respect. He had connections with God—we could see it in his life in our small community. And—perhaps just as important—he had connections with our parents.

Dave died last year, and though I hadn't seen him for a long time, memories of his face flooded my mind when I heard of his death. He was one of those people who affect you more than you realize at the time. I wrote to his wife, Jane, and thanked her for giving him up so many Saturday nights for my sake. She too will wear a crown in heaven.

As my youth group leader, Dave Thomas made a difference in my life just by being steady and faithful and consistently showing up. I work with young children at my church now, and I hope that one of them will one day look back and remember me as steady as mashed potatoes—just like Dave.

ACTION STEP

WHAT IS ONE AREA OF YOUR LIFE WHERE YOU KNOW YOU NEED A LITTLE HELP TO BECOME ALL THAT YOU CAN BE? WRITE THAT DOWN ON AN INDEX CARD. NOW LIST NAMES OF SEVERAL PEOPLE WHO HAVE SOMETHING TO TEACH YOU IN THIS AREA—YOUTH LEADERS, SISTERS, BROTHERS, TEACHERS. PRAY FOR THESE PEOPLE OVER THE NEXT WEEK AND ASK GOD TO LEAD YOU TO THE PERSON—WHETHER OR NOT THEY ARE ON THE LIST—WHO CAN HELP YOU GO TO THE NEXT LEVEL.

PRAYER

Dear Heavenly Father, thank You that You take an interest in Your children's growth and development as people. Please show me ways to grow and who can help me, and who I can help in return.

RELYING ON GOD

STRENGTH, DETERMINATION, AND SELF-RELIANCE AREN'T ENOUGH IN LIFE— WE MUST LEARN TO TRUST GOD.

Young man, young man,
your arm's too short to box with God.

JAMES WELDON JOHNSON

TO THINK ABOUT

- How much do you think you rely on God? All the time? During both good times and bad?
- Have you ever had to just watch and pray because there was nothing you could do to help a situation? How did it make you feel?
- How would your responses in both good and difficult times be different if you had a deeper faith in God?

LESSON FOR LIFE

PROMISES

God will...

Always be trustworthy
Hebrews 6:18-19

Be able to keep you from
stumbling in your faith
Jude 1:24

Protect those who listen
to Him
Proverbs 1:33

Work all situations for
your good
James 1:2, 4

Sometimes You Have to Pass the Ball

BIBLE STUDY PASSAGE: PHILIPPIANS 3:3-8

He chose what the world thinks is unimportant and what the world looks down on and thinks is nothing in order to destroy what the world thinks is important.

1 CORINTHIANS 1:28

Perhaps no basketball player is better known than Michael Jordan.   He entered in the NBA in 1984 and averaged 28.4 points as a rookie.   He led the league in scoring four of his first six seasons—but lacked what he wanted most, a championship. Interestingly, when he began scoring fewer points and depending more on others, he finally got what he most wanted.

So often in life, when we try to do everything in our own strength, things fall apart, leaving us miserable.   The good news is that with trust in God we are never powerless or helpless.

The Apostle Paul was a formidable character: He had his day's equivalent of two doctoral degrees (law and theology); he was a religious zealot who followed the letter of the law to a "t" (Philippians 3:6); he came from a wealthy and influential family (Philippians 3:5).   But it was when he discovered that

all his efforts and abilities weren't enough that he truly
became a powerful force for God. He helped spread the
Christian faith all over the world and turn it upside down.

    That's why he was quick to say, "The less I have, the more I
depend on Him" (2 Corinthians 12:10). That's why this great
orator would point out, "My teaching and preaching were not
with words of human wisdom that persuade people but with
proof of the power that the Spirit gives" (1 Corinthians 2:4).

    God has blessed you with gifts and talents to make a
difference in your world. But He's also created you with the
need to depend on Him consistently.

    Sometimes the greatest challenge in our lives is not to try
harder but to trust more.

> Be merciful to me, God;
> be merciful to me
> because I come to you
> for protection. Let me
> hide under the shadow
> of your wings until the
> trouble has passed.
> Psalm 57:1

REAL LIFE

The Day the Sea Parted Me

BILL COMSTOCK AS TOLD TO LANA COMSTOCK

A holiday with my sisters was like visiting a different planet. Me: ultra-cool guy from coastal California, raised by mother. Them: religious daughters of our minister father, raised in the sterile world of church meetings.

This visit, we were going river rafting. I worried they would think I was a total idiot when it came to religion, but I had heard enough to know there was a "big guy" upstairs. Was He necessary? I wasn't sure. My life was pretty good. The way I saw it, religious folks were drama queens in an uneventful world. I suppose if we lived in some Third-World country, it'd be different. Here in America, He wasn't in high demand.

We floated downriver in the hot Phoenix sun. Everybody was having a great time; this kind of thing was right up my alley. As we drifted along, I decided to hop out and take a dive from the rocky shore. Being the cautious daredevil that I was, I checked the depth of the water—shallow, but bottomless farther out. I thought through the mechanics of the dive and knew I had to stretch to hit deep.

On the cold rock, the dive commenced. It was perfection. Into the air I flew, and then—my body decided to "tuck." As I hit water, I wondered why, after all that foresight, did I change my plan? I'll never know. My scalp slid along the graveled river bottom and I chided myself. Standing up in the knee-deep water, I figured no harm done—just a little bruise in the morning. But then I heard the scream.

"Billllllll! Your head!" my sister yelled in terror.

I instinctively felt for damage. My hand sunk into open scalp and blood gushed, dyeing my tan shorts a bright, menacing red.

I probably should have been terrified, but God had other plans. My first thought was, *Well, this is where Jesus comes in.* A peaceful feeling chased away fear, pain, and worry as I prayed silently. The family was alarmed with good reason, but I was in a heavenly comfort zone. *So, this is why you need Him,* I thought. Stuff does happen, even in America, even to me. I was not as invincible as I once thought.

Our vehicle was parked several miles upstream. The nearest hospital was forty-five minutes away, with no plastic surgeon. I had no idea that out of the five layers protecting the brain, four of mine had been ripped open. One thin layer from death—like I said, God had other plans.

I made the drive with a sheet wrapped on my head, fully conscious. I couldn't help but laugh just a little—I knew I looked like something out of mummy movie. After Operation: Gravel Removal, I got 450 stitches. What an ordeal.

Did I begin to believe that day? No, I wasn't stupid—I'd always known He was there. Did I get to see faith in action? For sure. Now I understand everyone will eventually go through trauma—even in America. Trusting Him makes it much easier. I need God—every day. I also learned that I didn't need to wait to have 450 stitches to depend on God for everything!

ACTION STEP

WHAT ARE SOME SITUATIONS YOU ARE FACING THAT YOU SIMPLY DON'T HAVE THE STRENGTH AND WISDOM TO SOLVE ON YOUR OWN? HAVE YOU SPENT TIME IN PRAYER PUTTING THESE SITUATIONS INTO GOD'S HANDS, ASKING HIM TO DO WHAT YOU ARE UNABLE TO?

WHY NOT TAKE A LONG WALK, GET AWAY FROM THE DISTRACTIONS, AND SPEND AN HOUR IN PRAYER?

PRAYER

Father, it's sometimes hard for me to admit that I can't handle some things on my own. But the truth is that I do need You—all the time, in every situation. Please be near me today.

PRAYER

THROUGH PRAYER, GOD HAS PROVIDED A VERY SPECIAL WAY TO RELATE TO HIM AND SHARE OUR LIVES WITH HIM.

Prayer does not change God,
but it changes him who prays.

SØREN KIERKEGAARD

 ## TO THINK ABOUT

- Is prayer easy for you or difficult? Do you feel like you're really talking to God?
- What in your life distracts you most easily? Does that get in the way of you spending time in prayer?
- How would your life change if you spent even a little time each day in silent reflection before God?

LESSON FOR LIFE

PROMISES

God will...

Hear your prayers

2 Chronicles 7:14

Psalm 116:1-2

Do what's best for you

Romans 8:28

Reward your earnest

prayer

Matthew 7:7

Luke 18:1

Be near you when you

pray

James 4:8

Prayer Is Powerful

BIBLE STUDY PASSAGE: MATTHEW 21:18-22

Pray in the Spirit at all times with all kinds of prayers, asking for everything you need. To do this you must always be ready and never give up. Always pray for all God's people.

EPHESIANS 6:18

At the beginning of His ministry at age thirty, despite having so much to do in such a short amount of time for His Father in heaven, Jesus pulled away from everyone to spend forty days in the wilderness to pray and fast.   While alone, Jesus was tested three times by Satan, but each time answered the challenge with scripture and a profound sense of His purpose in life (Matthew 4:1-11).

Again, at the end of his earthly life, Jesus pulled away from the crowds to pray alone in the Garden of Gethsemane (Mark 14:35-36).   It was there, with the agony of the cross just before Him, that He reaffirmed His most earnest desire: "Not My will, but Yours, be done" (Luke 22:42 NKJV).

If Jesus Christ spent time in personal prayer, how much

more important is it for us?   We can come to the end of the day—or week or even month—and discover that we made no time at all to be alone with God.   Television, radio, school, practices, and other "noises" compete for our time and attention.

Jesus told His disciples, "If you ask me for anything in my name, I will do it" (John 14:14).   Prayer is powerful—but one of the ways we learn to pray as Jesus prayed, "Your will be done," is by spending time in prayer and silent reflection, taking time to really hear God's voice.   Plus, when God wants to use you to do something, He's most likely to be able to communicate that to you if you're spending regular time in prayer (John 15:4).

You don't have to take a forty-day trip to the desert to spend quiet time alone with God.   You can choose today to make prayer a higher priority in your life.   As you ask God to help you, He will prosper your prayer life—and your soul.

You did not choose me; I chose you.   And I gave you this work: to go and produce fruit, fruit that will last.   Then the Father will give you anything you ask for in my name.
John 15:16

REAL LIFE

In the Right Place at the Right Time

C. HOPE FLINCHBAUGH

In the middle of prayer and Bible reading on an ordinary morning, I suddenly heard a huge BANG.

"There's been an accident!" I heard my husband exclaim.

We rushed to the windows to see the front end of an old blue sports car wrapped around the telephone pole just off our property. Scott ran outside to help the victims while I called 911. Our young daughters watched the activity first from the windows and later from the front porch.

After calling the ambulance, I went outside, our cordless phone still in hand. A woman who taught at the local school district had stopped to help. Two high school girls were in the mangled car. The driver was okay. But by the time I reached the vehicle, the passenger, a beautiful young teen, had passed out and wouldn't waken. She didn't budge when I asked if she could hear me and gently touched her shoulder, but I saw that she was breathing. She was shivering and I gingerly placed my husband's coat over her.

I placed my hands near her shoulders and prayed for her healing and for peace, then said, "In the name of Jesus, wake up."

The girl's facial expression changed first. Her mouth moved. There was blood running out of the side. She opened her eyes and squinted up at us.

The teacher exclaimed, "I think that it was your prayer that did this!"

"Yes," I replied. "We serve a powerful God!"

I asked the driver what happened. The seventeen-year-old girl admitted to me that she and her girlfriend were supposed to be going to school, but had decided to cut class for the day.

I said, "Honey, do you realize you were on the wrong road going the wrong way and doing the wrong thing? You set yourself up for trouble when you didn't do what was right."

In tears she nodded, "I know, I know. We shouldn't have skipped school. My mom's going to kill me."

"Take it from a mama," I assured her fervently. "First, she'll be glad you're alive. Then she'll tell you about skipping school. And she should—she's your mother."

For the first time she gave a little laugh and nodded.

After the girls were transported to the hospital, I went inside and told my daughters what happened. And I thanked God for allowing me to be there to comfort them and pray for them—and for His amazing healing.

I think the greatest blessing I received that day was getting to hear God's voice. Our God is not a God made of stone that cannot hear or speak or see. He is alive and loves to talk to us, and will put us in the right place at the right time.

ACTION STEP

FASTING IS THE SPIRITUAL DISCIPLINE OF ABSTAINING FROM FOOD FOR A SET PERIOD OF TIME IN ORDER TO DEVOTE OUR HEARTS AND MINDS TO SPIRITUAL MATTERS. BUT NOT EATING IS NOT THE ONLY PHYSICAL EXPRESSION OF FASTING. CONSIDER A ONE-, TWO-, OR THREE-DAY PERIOD OF NO RADIO, TV, OR OTHER "NOISE" IN YOUR LIFE. REMEMBER, THE PURPOSE IS TO FOCUS OUR WHOLE HEART, SOUL, AND MIND ON GOD!

PRAYER

You speak to me through Your Word, and through pastors, and through books, but thank You, God, that You also speak to me in a quiet voice when I am silent before You. Thank You for the wonderful gift of prayer.

AUTHORITY

TO HONOR GOD, WE MUST HONOR THOSE IN AUTHORITY—EVEN WHEN WE DON'T TOTALLY AGREE OR UNDERSTAND.

The dream begins with a teacher who believes in you, who tugs and pushes and leads you to the next plateau, sometimes poking you with a sharp stick called "truth."

DAN RATHER

 TO THINK ABOUT

- ☞ Do you consider yourself a disciplined person?
- ☞ Have you ever been resistant to someone who "pushed" you—a parent or teacher who demanded more of you than you wanted to give?
- ☞ In what area of your life do you have the hardest time accepting authority?

LESSON FOR LIFE

PROMISES

God will...

Give you what you need
to do His will
Hebrews 13:20-21

Give you strength
Psalm 138:3

Love you consistently
Hosea 2:19

Discipline fairly
Psalm 119:75

Handling Authority

BIBLE STUDY PASSAGE: JOHN 15:15-27

Let your patience show itself perfectly in what you do.
Then you will be perfect and complete and will have
everything you need.

JAMES 1:4

You are at an age when parents, teachers, and others in authority actually want you to become more responsible for your own life. Most don't want to boss you around. However, there are right and wrong ways to become independent.

Before we get caught up on making all your own decisions, consider a few important points about authority—

- *Authority is necessary for humans to get along. To reject all authority is to reject necessary standards for individuals, societies, and even countries to peacefully coexist. "The ruler is God's servant to help you. But if you do wrong, then be afraid. He has the power to punish; he is God's servant to punish those who do wrong" (Romans 13:4).*
- *To resist authority is not always wrong. Jesus refused to follow*

the twisted teachings of the religious leaders of His day. If you are being asked to do something wrong, state your case as clearly, calmly, and positively as you can. If your appeal doesn't succeed, and the demand is truly wrong, ask God to guide you in the right way to "resist."

- Not all authorities are equal. Our society is filled with different "voices" claiming to speak truth. Who is right? Who do you believe? You are at an age when it is demanded of you to critically evaluate the different "messages" presented. The place to start is reading God's Word and learning to listen to His Spirit. Really get to know the Ultimate Authority.
- The more responsible you become, the less authority will be imposed on you. Put no boundaries on your life, and others will do it for you. If you live responsibly, parents and other authorities will more likely trust you to do what is right, without constantly "reminding" you how to act.
- We show love toward God when we submit to Him. Even the Son of God submitted. He claimed that this submission toward God proved His love for God. How much love toward God have you shown with your obedience? "I have obeyed my Father's commands, and I remain in his love.   In the same way, if you obey my commands, you will remain in my love" (John 15:10).

For the Lord's sake, yield to the people who have authority in this world: the king, who is the highest authority, and the leaders who are sent by him to punish those who do wrong and to praise those who do right.

1 Peter 2:13-14

163

REAL LIFE

Tough Love

STEPHEN A. PETERSON

Her name was Rita Clare, and she taught English Composition and Literature. She had a reputation for toughness—she gave pop quizzes, lots of homework, and lengthy term papers, and high grades were difficult to come by. Assigned to her class, I began my senior year filled with apprehension and fear.

Within a month after the fall period began, I grew to respect, admire, and regard Rita Clare as a true educator. One day, she asked me to stay after class.

I knew why she wanted to talk to me. It was to scold me for the poor performance I demonstrated in the composition portion of the course. For the remainder of the period, I thought through the possible scenarios I would face. Would she belittle my efforts? Would she tell me I was a hopeless case? What would she do to me? I asked God to let me die right there in class. But when the bell sounded, I was still alive.

Within seconds, the classroom had cleared of all but Rita Clare and me. Rather than face a brutal, mean teacher, I met with a kind teacher who gave an honest assessment of my performance and the steps needed to remediate my writing problems. She let me decide if I wanted to be helped or not.

From that day on, each Tuesday and Thursday, she and I went over parts of speech, grammar, sentence structure, and aspects of writing I never knew about. Sure, she was tough and the class and individual sessions difficult, but I quickly learned that she loved her subject and could inspire me to write even though I believed I had no ability to do so.

In the spring, I was assigned to Rita Clare's class once again. But her class was overloaded and some of us would have to be transferred. The other teachers were said to give few tests and the work was minimal—no term papers.

When the counselor asked who wanted to be assigned to another teacher, several students' hands went up. I noticed the fallen expression on Rita Clare's face, but I knew she was resilient and would not change her strategy for preparing students to articulate English in speaking and writing. I also knew of students who had graduated from her class and gone on to excel in the areas of literature and composition in college. I decided to remain with Rita Clare.

There were times I thought I wouldn't survive. I had to continue individual sessions to become a more proficient writer. When graduation day arrived, I thanked God for the opportunity to be in her class and for the quality of education I received. And when I entered my English and Composition class at Indiana University-Bloomington that fall, the professor said my writing skills were well above the rest of the class.

They call it "tough love," don't they? And for that privilege, I'll be tough skinned any day, month, or year when it comes to writing and dealing with life issues.

ACTION STEP

SELF-DISCIPLINE TAKES PRACTICE. CHOOSE AN AREA OF YOUR LIFE TO MASTER IN THE COMING WEEKS—TAKE RESPONSIBILITY TO KEEP YOUR ROOM CLEAN OR START AN EXERCISE OR READING PROGRAM. BE SURE TO PICK SOMETHING CHALLENGING AND OUTSIDE YOUR USUAL HABITS. ON A CALENDAR, PLOT OUT WHAT YOU'LL NEED TO DO EVERY DAY TO REACH YOUR GOAL, AND STICK WITH YOUR PLAN. WHEN YOU'RE DONE, REWARD YOURSELF WITH SOMETHING FUN AND CHOOSE A NEW GOAL!

PRAYER

Dear God, I trust You so much that I am willing to obey You in every area of my life. Please make me all that You want me to be.

NEGATIVE PEER PRESSURE

ALL OF US ARE INFLUENCED BY OTHERS, SO WE MUST CHOOSE OUR CLOSEST FRIENDS CAREFULLY.

Look carefully at the closest friends in your life,
for that is who you are becoming like.
ANONYMOUS

 To Think About

- Have you ever been negatively influenced by a friend? What happened?
- Why do you think it's so easy to be pulled away from God's path by certain friends?
- Do you consider yourself a positive influence on others?

LESSON FOR LIFE

PROMISES

God will...

Be your Friend
John 15:15

Never leave you
Hebrews 13:5

Be with you as you meet
with other believers
Matthew 18:20

Continue to work in you
Philippians 1:6

The Right Path

BIBLE STUDY PASSAGE: PSALM 1:1-6

Dear friends, since you already know about this, be careful. Do not let those evil people lead you away by the wrong they do. Be careful so you will not fall from your strong faith.

2 PETER 3:17

If you want to make good decisions in life, your first step is to avoid certain kinds of people, according to Psalm 1—

- *Don't hang around with the wicked: The word "wicked" is reserved for those who deliberately, joyfully, and maliciously do evil. If you have someone this destructive near your life, the best thing you can do is flee. Cut them off.*
- *Don't hang around sinners: We aren't to look down on people, even those who do wrong as a lifestyle. We must reach out to "lost" people with the love of God. But if you hang around other teens who aren't necessarily wicked, but who still can't stay out of trouble, you are setting yourself up to make bad decisions for your own life.*
- *Don't hang around scoffers: If you avoided everyone who is sarcastic at times, there might not be anyone left for you to be friends with!*

168

However, some people make it a habit to belittle, to "trash" everyone and everything. This kind of negative and cynical attitude is contagious. Don't catch it!

On the other hand, if you want to make good decisions, here are some great sources of help—

- *Hang onto God's Word: The Psalm writer says that blessed (happy) people "delight in the law of the Lord" (v. 2 NKJV). Solomon, the smartest man who ever lived, said: "These commands are like a lamp; this teaching is like a light. And the correction that comes from them will help you have life" (Proverbs 6:23).*
- *Hang around wise people: One of the best ways to live wisely is to interact with wise people. Solomon said, "Spend time with the wise and you will become wise, but the friends of fools will suffer" (Proverbs 13:20).*
- *Hang around godly people: Just as the wicked will tear you down, so the righteous will build you up. Solomon tells us "Good people take advice from their friends, but an evil person is easily led to do wrong" (Proverbs 12:26).*

The old adage tells us to choose our friends wisely. The best choice of friends you will ever make can begin today, when you say yes to being God's friend.

Do not be fooled: "Bad friends will ruin good habits."
1 Corinthians 15:33

REAL LIFE

Circle of Friends

ALEXANDRA A., AS TOLD TO T. SUZANNE ELLER

When I started seventh grade, I made some new friends. Although they cursed and teased people in a way that hurt them, I figured their behavior wouldn't affect me. I thought I was strong. I reasoned that instead of following in their footsteps, I might be able to influence them.

Wrong.

First I said a curse word. Then I started judging people for all the wrong reasons. This new me didn't happen all at once. Rather, I gradually changed as I spent more and more time with my friends.

One day, one person in the group persuaded several girls to bring Coke and rum to school, and before long they were bringing alcohol every day and drinking it in secret. They offered me the chance to drink, but I said no.

One day, some of the girls were drinking alcohol hidden in a soda bottle. A teacher passed and asked to see the bottle, and one girl threw it in the trash can. The teacher pulled it out, smelled the inside of the bottle, and made all of the girls follow him to the principal's office.

The girls who were caught told on everybody, and they were all suspended until further notice. The next night, their case was presented to the school board, and three people, including my best friend, were expelled from school. The others were suspended for two weeks.

Because I didn't drink the alcohol, I wasn't in trouble. I was the only one of my friends not suspended or expelled. I felt very alone walking through the halls without my friends.

Later that night, I asked God why He let this happen. What did I do to deserve losing my friends? Before I was through asking, God answered. The consequences of my friends' actions were meant to wake me up. I had turned into a follower. That night, I decided that I would focus more on God and what He wanted me to do with my life, rather than on what I wanted or what my friends thought.

Since my best friend was expelled, I started hanging out with one of the girls who had been suspended. We became pretty good friends, or at least I thought we did. That was before I found out that she'd been telling people that I was saying things behind their backs. The worst part is that they believed her. Girls walked by me and called me names. It was hard to wake up and go to school every morning.

I didn't have anyone to hang out with, and I had extra time on my hands. So I started reading the Bible, especially the Psalms. The whole book lifted my spirit—there were times when David felt alone, and yet he reached out to God. It made me realize that God would be with me as I finished the year without my friends.

My old friends helped me learn a life lesson: It is better to follow God instead of people. I have people in my life that I care about, but now God is the center of my circle of friends—and He's the best friend I've ever had.

ACTION STEP

TAKE A MINUTE TO ASSESS WHO YOU SPEND THE MOST TIME WITH. MAKE A LIST OF YOUR FRIENDS, AND ESTIMATE THE NUMBER OF HOURS PER WEEK YOU SPEND TALKING TO EACH ONE. WHO IS AT THE TOP OF THE LIST? DO YOU THINK YOUR SPIRITUAL GROWTH HAS BEEN HELPED OR HURT SINCE YOU STARTED SPENDING SO MUCH TIME WITH THAT PERSON? IS THERE ANYONE ON THE LIST YOU FEEL YOU'VE BEEN NEGLECTING? SEND THEM AN E-MAIL OR GIVE THEM A CALL TODAY.

PRAYER

Father, life is so hard without friends. Thank You for Your love and for the people You've put in my life, and please give me the courage to step away from hurtful friendships—even if it means being alone.

PARENTS' DIVORCE

WHEN FAMILIES BREAK UP, IT CREATES TREMENDOUS PAIN FOR EVERYONE, BUT GOD'S MERCY IS EVEN GREATER.

God is closest to those with broken hearts.

JEWISH SAYING

 TO THINK ABOUT

- Have you or a close friend experienced the pain of parents divorcing?
- What was hardest for you or your friend to understand?
- What helped you or your friend the most? Were you able to bless your friend during his or her hard time?

LESSON FOR LIFE

PROMISES

God will...

Hear your prayers and comfort you

Psalm 10:17

Enable you to comfort others

2 Corinthians 1:4

Bless you as you honor your parents

Ephesians 6:2-3

Be your Father

1 John 3:1

No More Sour Grapes

BIBLE STUDY PASSAGE:

In those days they shall say no more: "The fathers have eaten sour grapes, And the children's teeth are set on edge."

JEREMIAH 31:29 NKJV

Whether you come from a healthy, loving, godly family or a family that is filled with strife and brokenness, the following principles will help you be blessed—and be a blessing—

- *Pray for your parents: "I tell you to pray for all people, asking God for what they need and being thankful to him" (1 Timothy 2:1). Even though you are the "kid" and your parents are the "grownups," it doesn't mean that they are immune from temptation and don't struggle. Ask God to give your parents and your entire family more faith, peace, kindness, love, and grace.*
- *Honor your parents: "Children, obey your parents as the Lord wants, because this is the right thing to do" (Ephesians 6:1). You are a truly blessed person if your parents are together and love God, you, and each other. But even if your parents have significant problems, it pleases God when you honor them. He promises you a long, healthy life in return (Exodus 20:12).*

- *Learn from your parents: "Wise children take their parents' advice, but whoever makes fun of wisdom won't listen to correction" (Proverbs 13:1). Unfortunately because so many adults are divorced today, we sometimes have to learn what not to do. But positively, God will give you special insights and wisdom when you listen carefully and seriously to your parents.*
- *Don't take blame for your parents' problems: "At that time people will no longer say: 'The parents have eaten sour grapes, and that caused the children to grind their teeth from the sour taste'" (Jeremiah 31:29). In the Old Testament, the people believed that the son had to pay for his father's sin; that he was just as responsible for it as his dad. You can show utmost love and respect for your parents, but they will answer to God for their live and actions—and they will answer to God for their life and actions.*
- *Love your parents: "Most importantly, love each other deeply, because love will cause many sins to be forgiven" (1 Peter 4:8). Paul tells us that the three greatest dynamics in the world are faith, hope, and love, but the greatest is love. Perfect or imperfect, you will bless your parents—and yourself—by loving them!*

The Lord is close to the brokenhearted, and he saves those whose spirits have been crushed.

Psalm 34:18

175

REAL LIFE

Put 'er There, Pal

I met Kimberly at a senior high camp in the Southwest several years ago. Sixteen. Cute. Smiling. Friendly.

Following the Wednesday evening chapel service, she intercepted me as I walked toward the back of the meeting room. Her smile was gone, replaced with a frown; a gray cloud had settled over her sunny disposition.

She asked if I had a moment to talk. I told her I did, and we sat down on the back row. She paused as a small group of smiling, jostling, chattering friends flittered past. Her lips quivered, her eyes teared, and she buried her head on my shoulder as she began to sob.

I wondered if a boyfriend had broken up with her recently, or if some other crisis had occurred. The intensity of her tears made me wonder what was coming.

"The night before I left for camp," said Kimberly when she could finally talk, "my dad stopped by my room. I was packing. He stuck out his hand and said, 'Put 'er there, pal.' So I shook his hand.

"Then he said, 'When you get home from camp, I won't be here. I'm leaving your mother. Just thought I'd say so long. It might be awhile before we see each other again.'"

I felt miserable for this sixteen-year-old young lady, no longer smiling, no longer sunny. She'd been hiding a painful secret the last few days behind a wave and a smile.

"My dad used to be a Christian," she continued. "Something happened to him several years ago, and he's never been the same. He quit giving my mom and sister and me any kind of love and affection. We all knew he would leave sooner or later if something didn't change. It's kind of a relief. I just wish that he could have hugged me and said he loved me when he said good-bye," she choked out miserably.

She cried. I cried. The others who joined us cried. We all talked. We all hugged. She asked if I would remember to pray for her. I promised I would. I wrote her name on a prayer list I keep in my Bible. Her name is still there, and I still pray for her.

Whenever I pray for her, I pray for the teens and the adults of her church, that they would realize a lovely young lady needs their support. She needs people with listening hearts to help her work through some painful days.

Every time I see Kimberly's name, I wonder if she has found the healing God so often brings through the embrace of others. I hope so.

ACTION STEP

MARRIAGE IS A LONG WAYS INTO YOUR FUTURE, BUT IT'S STILL OKAY TO PRAY FOR YOUR FUTURE MARRIAGE PARTNER. ASK GOD TO BLESS THEM AND PROTECT THEM FROM EVIL AND HARM. ASK GOD TO HELP YOU BECOME THE PERSON HE WANTS YOU TO BE.

PRAYER

Lord God, thank You that You are able to work all things for good. Please guide my parents and me—help me interact with them in a way that pleases You.

JEALOUSY

WHEN WE LOVE OURSELVES AS GOD LOVES US, WE CAN SLAY THE GREEN-EYED MONSTER OF ENVY IN OUR LIVES.

Jealousy is simply and clearly the fear that you do not have value. Jealousy scans for evidence to prove the point—that others will be preferred and rewarded more than you. There is only one alternative—self-value.

JENNIFER JAMES

 TO THINK ABOUT

- Do you find it easy to be happy for others and celebrate their successes?   Or do you feel envious?
- Do you often find yourself complaining and being critical of others?   Is the problem their actions or your attitude?
- If you loved yourself more, how would your life and attitude toward others change?

LESSON FOR LIFE

PROMISES

God will...

Hear your prayers
Mark 11:24-25

Think you're important
Matthew 10:29-31

Use you, no matter how
insignificant you feel
1 Corinthians 1:27-29

Accept you
Galatians 2:16

Green-Eyed Monster

BIBLE STUDY PASSAGE: JAMES 4:1-10

Each person should judge his own actions and not compare himself with others. Then he can be proud for what he himself has done.

GALATIANS 6:4

Have you ever been bitten by the green-eyed monster called jealousy? When we let jealousy creep or roar into our souls, we hurt ourselves—including our relationship with God—and others in a number of ways—

- *We are always competing: "Let us walk properly, as in the day, not in revelry and drunkenness, not in lewdness and lust, not in strife and envy" (Romans 13:13 NKJV). Sure it's good to do our best. We want good grades. We want to win at tennis. We want to strive for excellence and sometimes that means competition. But when we let competition dominate our relationships, strife and hurt feelings will always be the result.*
- *We are always comparing: "Each person should judge his own actions and not compare himself with others. Then he can be*

180

proud for what he himself has done" (Galatians 6:4). If God created you the way you are for a reason; if He loves you for who you are; if He has a plan and purpose for your life; why would you want to be like someone else? It's almost the same as saying others have a better idea for your life than God does.

- *We are always criticizing and complaining: "Do everything without complaining or arguing" (Philippians 2:14). If you find yourself constantly criticizing others, guess what? They might not be the real problem. The real problem might be your feelings of jealousy. What causes jealousy? Often it is feelings of inferiority. No wonder Jesus says "Love your neighbor as you love yourself" (Matthew 22:39). Once we love ourselves, we no longer feel the need to trash others.*

The best antidote to jealousy is to affirm your belief in God and that He has a purpose for you. As you let your soul find rest in Him, you'll find that you compare yourself with others less and less.

Peace of mind means a healthy body, but jealousy will rot your bones.
Proverbs 14:30

181

REAL LIFE

Congratulations, Becky

JESSICA INMAN

One of my favorite magazines had arrived in the mail. I flipped through it, starting at the back like I always did. I frantically turned two pages forward, though, when I recognized a familiar name: Becky Campbell.*

I'd known Becky for a while—we shared a common interest in writing. There in my magazine was an article she'd written about her experience with an eating disorder.

I quickly read it. It was good—really good. And all of a sudden, my stomach was weighted with a realization: I was jealous. I'd only written a few things here and there, and had actually gotten rejected when I submitted something to this same magazine.

I didn't want to feel jealous, but I did. I prayed, "God, I really must confess that I'm just jealous. I don't know what to do."

I'm capable of being a pretty jealous person. It had cost me a friendship last year—I just couldn't seem to get over my jealousy of one girl because I felt like someone somewhere was writing up an evaluation of both of us, and I was found wanting. I've heard it said that jealousy comes from insecurity—and I guess I find that to be true.

I usually ended up channeling the anger that came from feeling second best toward whoever was the object of my jealousy. Not good. And not pleasing to

God.   So I had determined that I was going to deal with my jealousy.

I prayed that God would bless my relationships and help me love people.   I made a list of things about me that were special: I liked learning, I had an extensive knowledge of music trivia, I was kind to people, and I liked to write.

I told myself that I didn't have to be the best at these things, as long as I let God use me in those areas.   This made it easier anytime another girl sang a solo or sank a free throw and seemed to have the attention of the whole world.   Before long, it had been a while since I felt jealous.

Now, with Becky's article, it was all coming to a test.

I didn't think about the article for a while, letting it fade into the background my busy day.   Later, though, I went outside and sat on the patio.

It was like God was talking to me.   *You know Becky has an important story that needs to be told.   You know she really did a good job.   You know that doesn't mean you're not good at what you do.*

All true.   I also knew I could let jealousy go.   God would give me opportunities to use my gifts for Him, and He had recently done for Becky.   All was as it should be.

When I came inside, I wrote Becky an e-mail, congratulating her on a great article.   As I hit "send," I truly wanted her to be encouraged, and I thanked God for changing my heart.

*Names have been changed.

ACTION STEP

SIT DOWN AND MAKE A LIST OF THE THINGS THAT MAKE YOU UNIQUE—YOU LOVE MUSIC, YOU'RE GOOD AT BASKETBALL, YOU LIKE TO TALK TO OLDER PEOPLE, YOU'RE A GOOD COOK. PLACE YOUR LIST SOMEWHERE YOU'LL SEE IT OFTEN.

PRAYER

Lord God, please forgive me for allowing jealousy to take hold of my heart and hurt my relationships. Please help me find my strength in You today and to bless the people around me.

HELPING OTHERS

WHEN WE JOYFULLY RECEIVE GOD'S BLESSINGS, OUR JOY SPILLS OVER AND BLESSES OTHERS.

*We cannot hold a torch to light another's path
without brightening our own.*

BEN SWEETLAND

TO THINK ABOUT

- ☞ When have you been blessed by another person's joy?
- ☞ Have you blessed others because of your joyful love for God?
- ☞ What are some specific ways you can share God's joy with others more often?

LESSON FOR LIFE

PROMISES

God will...

Help you

Psalm 28:7

Bless you as you bless others

Hebrews 6:10

Matthew 10:42

Prepare you for good works

Ephesians 2:10

Bless you and give you peace

Numbers 6:24-26

My Cup Runneth Over

BIBLE STUDY PASSAGE: 2 CORINTHIANS 9:6-11

I taught you to remember the words Jesus said: "It is more blessed to give than to receive."

ACTS 20:35

One of the greatest—but most neglected—sources of joy and blessings in our lives is through bringing joy and blessing to others.   Despite the various studies that prove the happiest people in the world are those who serve others, people don't seem to be volunteering to serve their communities as much as they used to.

Jesus taught His disciples that it is more blessed to give than to receive.   One obvious—but easily forgotten—reason is that if you are giving to others, it implies you have something to give in the first place!   Most of us can count many blessings in our lives right now.   But can we just as easily count the number of ways that we bless others?

In Deuteronomy 16, the children of Israel are reminded to come before the Lord to worship.   Three yearly feasts had been established as special times to grow closer to God.   Passover, the subject of chapter 16, was to be celebrated at the beginning of the year to remind the Israelites that God had delivered Israel from oppression and slavery (Exodus 12:2). What a blessing! One of the clear expectations when the people attended the feast was spelled out in verse 17: As God has blessed you, bring a gift of gratitude to bless God and others. Everyone is not asked to bring the same or an equal gift, but to give according to what God has given them.

Have you been blessed? It is wonderful to serve a God who wants to bless you, but let's not forget to bless others in equal measure.

Those who give one of these little ones a cup of cold water because they are my followers will truly get their reward.
Matthew 10:42

REAL LIFE

Terrified on Timpanogos Mountain

ANDREW LORENZ

On a warm, sunny afternoon outside Salt Lake City, my mom and I chugged up Timpanogos Mountain for a cave tour. A sign at the ticket station warned us of the one-and-a-half-mile hike up to the cave, an unforgiving trail with a steep grade that shouldn't be attempted by people with heart or respiratory problems. Bring it on, I thought.

After an hour of huffing and puffing, we reached the cave. Mom plopped onto a bench next to a man wearing a beige worksuit. He looked like a park employee, and Mom thought he was our tour guide.

But he wasn't an employee—he was on the tour. It had taken him almost three hours to climb up the mountain, and he was exhausted. His name was Emilio and he was originally from Madrid, as evidenced by his thick accent.

After exploring the beautiful winding caves, we stepped back outside. Only it wasn't sunny anymore—thick black clouds and strong wind had taken over. My stomach flipped over as I thought about climbing down the mountain in a storm.

I charged on, nervous and eager to go home, but Mom waited for Emilio. "Mom! Hurry up!" I yelled. "I see lightning!"

I waited next to a sign that said blue lines on the trail meant rock slides were likely in those areas. Just great—here I was dodging lightning and rocks, and Mom was dragging her feet.

When she finally caught up to us, she panted, "We have to wait for Emilio."

"Why? You know how long it'll take with him! I can't stand this!"

"Andrew, please. He could fall or have a heart attack from exhaustion." She put her hands on my shoulders. "Andrew, you're strong, and a little shorter than Emilio. Would you let him put his hands on your shoulders from behind for support?"

I looked back up the path at Emilio. He was bent over, panting for breath. I relented. "Okay. I'll do it."

He could only take about twenty steps before he had to rest his poor knees, so we baby-stepped down the path, rain pelting our backs. As we walked, he taught me Spanish and told me about his life in Madrid, about his Cuban wife, how he'd worked as an auditor on a Norwegian ship. Sometime during the three hours we spent glued to each other down that steep, slippery path, I started to like this old guy.

Ten feet before we reached the bottom, Emilio pulled away from me and stood tall by himself. "I do the last steps myself!"

We cheered when Emilio reached level ground. Mom hugged him. He shook my hand and said, "Andrew, you are a fine young man. Thank you for your help."

I knew I would miss Emilio. I'd learned something that day. From that first moment Emilio put his hands on my shoulders for support, I wasn't afraid of the storm anymore. What I learned is that when you help somebody you forget your own fears.

ACTION STEP

HOW HAVE YOU BEEN BLESSED? DO YOU HAVE A PARTICULAR TALENT? A GREAT FAMILY LIFE? MATERIAL BLESSINGS? THINK OF A WAY TO SHARE YOUR BLESSINGS WITH OTHERS. SING AT A NURSING HOME. VOLUNTEER TO HELP COACH A YMCA BASKETBALL OR VOLLEYBALL LEAGUE. INVITE A FRIEND OVER FOR DINNER WHO MIGHT BE STRUGGLING AT HOME OR SCHOOL. WHATEVER YOU CHOOSE TO DO, DO SO WITH GRATITUDE FOR GOD'S BLESSINGS.

PRAYER

Thank You, Heavenly Father, for the many ways You have met my needs and bless me so richly. Give me a joyful gratitude that spills those blessings into the lives of others.

RENEWING YOUR MIND

WHAT IS IN OUR MINDS INFLUENCES HOW WE ACT—SO IT'S CRUCIAL THAT WE PROVIDE OUR THOUGHT LIFE WITH POSITIVE NOURISHMENT

*Every morning I spend fifteen minutes
filling my mind full of God; and so
there's no room left for worry thoughts.*

HOWARD CHANDLER CHRISTY

TO THINK ABOUT

- Are you happy with your thought life—or are there some things you'd like to change?
- Why do you think our thoughts have so much impact on the way we live our lives?
- What do you think is the best way to cleanse your thought life?

191

LESSON FOR LIFE

PROMISES

God will...

Keep working in you
Philippians 1:6

Renew you
Ephesians 4:22-23

Value you
Deuteronomy 26:18

Be there to help you
Ephesians 3:12

Pure Minds in an R-Rated World

BIBLE STUDY PASSAGE: EPHESIANS 5:15-20

For as he thinks in his heart, so is he.

PROVERBS 23:7 NKJV

It's tough to keep a pure mind in our culture. We're constantly slammed with images and words that go against what we know is good and right. Renewing our minds is a tough battle, but it's absolutely necessary. Once we lose control of our thoughts, we often lose control of our behavior. We can see a huge difference in the way we think by—

• *Committing ourselves to God: "So brothers and sisters, since God has shown us great mercy, I beg you to offer your lives as a living sacrifice to him. Your offering must be only for God and pleasing to him, which is the spiritual way for you to worship. Do not change yourselves to be like the people of this world, but be changed within by a new way of thinking. Then you will be able to decide what God wants for you; you will know what is good and pleasing to him and what is perfect" (Romans 12:1-2). When you declare that God comes first in your life, your mindset*

192

automatically begins to change. You immediately are less selfish. You're not as comfortable with certain kinds of negative and profane thoughts, either.

- Getting rid of negative messages: "But now also put these things out of your life: anger, bad temper, doing or saying things to hurt others, and using evil words when you talk" (Colossians 3:8). Garbage in; garbage out. Whatever we feed our mind is what ends up working itself out in our spirit and behavior. Just as Joseph fled from temptation (Genesis 39:12), so you must flee from certain negative images and words.
- Filling our minds with good thoughts: "Brothers and sisters, think about the things that are good and worthy of praise" (Philippians 4:8). It's tough not to think about certain things when you're trying not to think about them! The key is to replace bad thoughts with good ones.
- Being filled with the Spirit: "Do not be drunk with wine, which will ruin you, but be filled with the Spirit. Speak to each other with psalms, hymns, and spiritual songs, singing and making music in your hearts to the Lord" (Ephesians 5:18-19). When we turn our lives over to God, the Holy Spirit comes to live inside us. But we must still ask Him to take control of everything—including our thought life—to experience a total life change.

Do not change yourselves to be like the people of this world, but be changed within by a new way of thinking. Then you will be able to decide what God wants for you; you will know what is good and pleasing to him and what is perfect.

Romans 12:2

REAL LIFE

Peace of Mind

I grew up in a nice Christian home.   We weren't rich or poor, but my parents were generous with us kids and others.   We had a nice house in the suburbs and a nice church to attend.

So how in the world did I get into so much trouble?   I became sexually active at age fourteen.   I started taking drugs at age fifteen.   My grades plummeted. I got kicked off the football team.   I got in fights.   I constantly defied my parents.   I was picked up by the police numerous times, but somehow avoided an official "record."

Then one day, leaning against a rack of baseball bats in the sports equipment room at school, I had a coach get in my face.   He let me know my life needed to change.   He didn't mince words letting me know what a waste I was making of myself.   He reminded me that I had been raised better and needed to get right with God.

I did.   And man, what an incredible change took place in my life.   My parents, sisters, teachers, and friends at church were thrilled. I was no longer angry and rebellious.

However, I did have a couple of problems.   Even though I felt God's incredible love in my heart, there were two things I couldn't shake loose of: bad language and a ton of lust.

I told guys on the baseball team I was saved now, but then I'd cuss up a storm, using every word in the book. I also couldn't keep my eyes off sexy images and was constantly tempted to fool around with the girls I dated.

I finally discovered through the help of my youth pastor that temptation will always be with us, but it's worse when we feed it with old patterns of behaving and thinking.

Call me crazy, but I had to get rid of some things. First was some of my music. A lot of what I listened to was just too angry and sexual for my good. Second, I had to stop going to R-rated and many PG-13 movies. They put too many thoughts in my head. And I definitely had to cut out late night channel surfing for the same reason.

I basically had to get my mind thinking new thoughts. I started listening to Christian music and reading my Bible. Slowly but surely, my old thoughts began to be replaced with new ones—better ones. Before long, it had been a while since I said a curse word or lingered too long on a racy TV program.

Thinking better thoughts changed the way I felt during the day. Considering all the things I gave up, you'd think I'd feel like I was missing out on stuff, but as it turned out, I was much happier. It also became easier to deal with temptation—my dates were more fun when I didn't have such deep temptations nagging me.

It took a while to clear the junk out of my mind, but it was so worth it. And it's still a process, an everyday battle to renew my mind, but it's worth the effort to have the peace and wholeness that having a clean mind brings.

ACTION STEP

WHAT NEGATIVE WORDS AND IMAGES DO YOU ALLOW TO ENTER YOU SOUL ON A CONSISTENT BASIS? WRITE DOWN TWO THINGS CURRENTLY IN YOUR LIFE THAT YOU NEED TO AVOID. AND THEN WRITE DOWN NEW THINKING PATTERNS THAT YOU NEED TO ADD TO YOUR LIFE.

PRAYER

Heavenly Father, help me to think about the world the same You do—with love and compassion and purity.

SELF-ESTEEM

YOUR ABILITY TO EXPRESS LOVE TO OTHERS IS LINKED TO YOUR ABILITY TO LOVE YOURSELF.

God loves and cares for us,
even to the least event
and smallest need of life.

HENRY EDWARD MANNING

TO THINK ABOUT

- What are some of the negative consequences of low self-esteem?
- What have been some of the determining factors in your ability to love yourself—or in your struggle to love yourself?
- How do you believe God views you? Do you accept His love?

LESSON FOR LIFE

PROMISES

God will...

Accept you and justify you
Romans 3:30

Help you during times of
trial and temptation
Hebrews 4:15

Be compassionate to
those who are struggling
Matthew 12:20

Hear you when you ask
for help
Psalm 6:9

Lead His people when
they are weak in faith
Isaiah 40:11

The Woman at the Well

BIBLE STUDY PASSAGE: 4:4-26

The Lord did not care for you and choose you because there were many of you—you are the smallest nation of all. But the Lord chose you because he loved you, and he kept his promise to your ancestors.

DEUTERONOMY 7:7-8

If ever there was a person who had reasons to struggle with their self-image, it was the woman who met Jesus at the well as recorded in John 4—

- *First of all, she was a Samaritan. In Jesus' day, the Jews despised all Samaritans as religious infidels and "half breeds." When Israel was conquered by the Babylonians in 586 B.C., the youngest and most educated were taken into captivity. When their descendants returned to Jerusalem seventy years later, they expected to find a thriving center of worship and faith. Instead, many who had been left behind converted to other religions and married people from other countries. They were despised from that moment on.*
- *Second, she was a woman, which meant she had second-class status*

in her culture and was viewed as the "property" of her husband.

- *Third, she had failed at love. Jesus asked her where her husband was. She admitted she wasn't married, but was living with a man. Jesus pointed out she had previously been married six times! Whether a serial widow or divorcee, she had probably given up on marital vows.*
- *Fourth, she was rejected by her peers. Jesus met her during the hottest time of the day with no one else around her. The women of Middle East villages gathered water at the well together during the coolest part of the day.*

If anyone had reason to feel bad about themselves and their lot in life, it was this Samaritan woman. But when Jesus entered her life, everything changed. He took the initiative and spoke to her first, uncommon for a man to do in that culture. In the same way, He reaches out to us long before we reach toward Him. He looked at her as a person on the basis of her potential—not her past or even her present circumstances. Most importantly, He offered her a living water that would satisfy the emptiness and longing of her soul, a drink of water that would provide renewal for her parched soul and life.

Even if you feel as needy as a lonely Samaritan at a well today, be assured that Jesus provides you with all the reasons you need to love and embrace yourself.

In my trouble I called to the Lord. I cried out to my God for help. From his temple he heard my voice; my call for help reached his ears.

Psalm 18:6

REAL LIFE

Why Me?

CANDACE MARRA

It had been a long time since Daniel had prayed. As if it wasn't already difficult enough to live in poverty with an abusive, alcoholic father, he also had juvenile diabetes, a condition he'd battled since he was three. His peers ruthlessly taunted him. *Why me, God?* he used to pray. *Why can't I just be normal?*

As he got older, Daniel's diabetes had grown worse along with his father's abusive behavior. Daniel had accepted Jesus as his Savior, but often found himself wondering if God really cared. Life was hard, and God seemed so far away. At age thirteen, he gave up on God altogether. If God wasn't going to help him, he would go his own way, smoking pot and getting into trouble.

Now he faced life with diabetes, and without his mother. His mom left his dad that year. The abuse had stopped, but his diabetes continued to run out of control. His high school was no longer willing to accept the liability for Daniel's condition, so he wasn't even allowed to attend school. It seemed like everything was against him.

What he didn't realize was that even though he wasn't praying anymore, his aunt Glinda prayed for him daily. And God began answering those prayers even while Daniel lived in rebellion.

At age fourteen, he attended a diabetes camp, where he met other teens with diabetes. Through an administrative glitch, Daniel was placed in a dorm full of older high school boys. They treated him like a little brother, something he'd never experienced. He saw for the first time that he wasn't alone in his sickness, and that others could care about him and accept him just for who he was.

God wasn't through working in Daniel's life. Although he was no longer able to attend school, he graduated with a full diploma from an alternative education program. Soon after, his Aunt Glinda took him into her home. Daniel began to feel the pull of the Holy Spirit.

He attended church with Aunt Glinda and was especially moved when an evangelist came for a five-night revival. Daniel saw God minister powerfully to many individuals during those five nights, and on the last night, he asked for forgiveness and gave his life back to God. He had seen how God had quietly but obviously poured His love into Daniel's life, and he wanted to thank Him.

Now Daniel looks forward to the day when he himself will be a preacher of the gospel, offering hope to many.

If he had the chance to live his life over again, he would not change a thing, not even the diabetes. He believes that everything is part of God's plan, and that what the devil meant for evil, God is going to turn around for good. He believes his past is going to help him to be sensitive to the needs of others as he ministers to them.

Daniel has learned to love and value himself because God loves and values him.

ACTION STEP

YOU'VE WRITTEN LETTERS TO OTHERS AS A WAY TO AFFIRM YOUR LOVE FOR AND BELIEF IN THEM. WRITE A LETTER TO YOURSELF, REMINDING YOU OF HOW MUCH GOD LOVES YOU—AND YOUR OWN SENSE OF SELF APPRECIATION. TUCK IT ANYWHERE YOU CAN READ IT AS A REMINDER OF THIS SOUL MATTER.

PRAYER

Thank You, God, for being the One who believes in me and loves me as no one else ever could. You see in my heart and declare me beautiful.

GOD SPEAKS TO US

WHEN WE SLOW DOWN AND LISTEN, WE CAN HEAR GOD'S VOICE.

Prayer is not monologue, but dialogue.
God's voice in response to mine
is its most essential part.

ANDREW MURRAY

 To THINK ABOUT

- ⚷ Have you ever sensed that God was speaking directly to your heart?
- ⚷ What are the different ways that God speaks to us?
- ⚷ How can you be a better listener in your prayer life?

LESSON FOR LIFE

PROMISES

God will...

Call you by name
John 10:3

Work on your heart
Philippians 2:13

Prepare you
2 Timothy 2:21

Guide you
Psalm 32:8

A Whisper in the Night

BIBLE STUDY PASSAGE: 1 SAMUEL 3:1-10

Speak, Lord. I am your servant and I am listening.

1 SAMUEL 3:10

Sometimes we are accused of hearing only what we want to hear. We hear our mom telling us she'll take us shopping this weekend, but not that we need to empty the dishwasher. The same might be said in our spiritual lives. How closely do we listen for God's voice to lead and direct us?

God speaks to everyone through His Word. Everything we need to know about loving Him and others is clearly spelled out there. But sometimes God speaks in special ways, under special circumstances, with a special message to us individually.

God speaks to us through—

- *Our own thoughts—if we read His Word and talk to Him in prayer, it shouldn't surprise us when we begin coming up with ideas that seem heaven-sent. "Lord, every morning you hear my voice. Every morning, I tell you what I need, and I wait for your answer" (Psalm 5:3).*
- *The thoughts of others—again, if we talk about God with others*

who know Him and love Him, we should expect to hear His voice in the words of a trusted friend. "A good person speaks with wisdom, and he says what is fair" (Psalm 37:30).

- A question or problem that won't go away—often, when we sense a special need in our community or in our own life, God is prompting us to discover something He wants us to do about it through us. We are often His answers to others' prayers. God called Paul to Macedonia by giving him a vision of a Macedonian man begging for help (Acts 16:9-10).

- A sermon or song—when we go to church with an open heart and mind, we should expect to hear a special word from God through the music and preaching. "Come, let us go up to the mountain of the Lord, to the Temple of the God of Jacob. Then God will teach us his ways, and we will obey his teachings" (Isaiah 2:3).

- A still, small voice—though people might think we're crazy, it's true that God does directly impress His thoughts on our minds today. Even as He called Samuel to be His prophet in the still of the night (1 Samuel 3:4), sometimes He chooses to make himself known directly on our hearts.

The real question is not whether God speaks today, but how well do we listen?

The Lord says, "I will make you wise and show you where to go. I will guide you and watch over you."
Psalm 32:8

REAL LIFE

Just What I Needed

KRISTINE ABBOTT AS TOLD TO JESSICA INMAN

I was thrilled when my sister and her family came to live with us for a while. It gave me three new "sisters"—my sister's kids are all really close to my age, and we always had fun together.

But things got scary when my oldest niece, three years older than me, started getting sick. The doctors knew Misti had some kind of problem with her colon, but they couldn't figure out what was wrong. Then came surgeries. And more surgeries, where the doctors found really bad cuts on her insides.

She couldn't go to school or anything—she missed pretty much her whole tenth grade year. It made her upset and angry, and she felt distant from God, which really worried me.

What if she left God? I hated seeing her frustrated and confused. And I hated seeing her in pain and unable to do the things she wanted to do—she was special to me. I believed it was all my fault. It had to be—it happened right after she moved here. Plus, I had been distant from God. Maybe He was punishing me and the only thing He could do was make Misti sick.

I didn't tell anyone I was thinking like this. I didn't even pray about it at first—I just kept it to myself. Eventually, though, I just couldn't take it anymore. I felt anxious and guilty. I asked God to bring me someone I could talk to and know they knew what I was talking about.

After Misti came back from a specialist in Ohio, I felt better. She came back a little happier, and I thought surely the doctors knew what they were doing. I still felt detached from God, though. After a while, I started praying again—I was glad Misti was doing better, but I still really wanted someone to talk to.

Then I went on a retreat with my youth group. The games and activities were great, and I was with people I knew and liked. In chapel, though, when we sang songs and listened to the speaker talk about God, I just felt so numb.

I went down to the altar to pray with a friend of mine. When chapel ended, I was sitting there chatting with one of the leaders, someone who knew Misti and knew about everything she'd been going through. I fidgeted with the carpet on the stage, thinking about what I was going to say. Finally, I blurted out that I blamed God and me for what had happened to Misti.

She told me that God allows things in our lives, but that He still cares for us and will be extra close to us through the hard times. It was as if God was speaking directly to me through her. Just hearing her say that, I suddenly felt better: It wasn't my fault, and I could trust God and lean on Him when things got crazy.

God had answered my prayer. I thanked Him that He had given me someone to talk to, someone to help comfort me.

When I saw Misti again, I gave her a big hug. I knew that God would take care of her and me, and He'll help me be there for her when she needs me.

ACTION STEP

JAMES SAYS OF WISDOM THAT "IF ANY OF YOU NEEDS WISDOM, YOU SHOULD ASK GOD FOR IT. HE IS GENEROUS AND ENJOYS GIVING TO ALL PEOPLE, SO HE WILL GIVE YOU WISDOM. BUT WHEN YOU ASK GOD, YOU MUST BELIEVE AND NOT DOUBT. ANYONE WHO DOUBTS IS LIKE A WAVE IN THE SEA, BLOWN UP AND DOWN BY THE WIND" (VV. 5-6). WHEN WAS THE LAST TIME YOU SPECIFI-CALLY ASKED GOD TO SPEAK TO YOU ABOUT A PARTICULAR STRUGGLE? A RELA-TIONSHIP ISSUE? YOUR FUTURE? YOUR SERVICE TO HIM AND OTHERS?

YOU'VE PROBABLY EXPERIENCED A RETREAT WITH YOUR YOUTH GROUP—A TIME TO JUST GET AWAY FROM YOUR ROUTINE AND LISTEN TO GOD. WHY NOT TAKE A MINI RETREAT TODAY—A FULL HOUR AWAY FROM TV AND MUSIC TO JUST PRAY? FIND A QUIET PLACE AND GO FOR IT!

PRAYER

God of the universe, I'm amazed that You speak to us so quietly and so often. Thank You for Your love. Please soften my heart and give me ears to hear You today.

GOD'S DELIVERANCE

GOD HEARS THE PRAYERS OF THOSE WHO CALL TO HIM FOR MERCY.

This is sane, wholesome, practical, working faith: That it is a man's business to do the will of God; second, that God himself takes on the care of that man; and third, that therefore that man ought never to be afraid of anything.

GEORGE MACDONALD

TO THINK ABOUT

- Have you ever felt forgotten by God? Like He wasn't really working in your life?
- What situation are you praying about today?
- Why do you think we sometimes have to wait for God to accomplish something in our lives?

LESSON FOR LIFE

PROMISES

God will...

Make you blameless
Colossians 1:22

Take sole responsibility
for vengeance
Romans 12:19

Forgive you as you
forgive others
Matthew 6:14-15

Hold On

BIBLE STUDY PASSAGE: GENESIS 50:15-26

You meant to hurt me, but God turned your evil into good
to save the lives of many people, which is being done.

GENESIS 50:20

God promised to make Abraham the father of a great nation, with descendants as numerous as the stars in the sky (Genesis 15:5). Despite his great faith, can you blame him for questioning when this was going to happen when he was still fatherless at age seventy-five (Genesis 12:4)?

Samuel anointed David as king of Israel in response to Saul's spirit of disobedience (1 Samuel 16:1). The problem was that David was hunted like a fugitive for the next seven years (1 Samuel 19:9). No wonder he cried to God, "Why have you forgotten me? Why am I sad and troubled by my enemies?" (Psalm 42:9).

Moses led the Hebrew slaves from captivity into the Promised Land—over the course of forty years (Exodus 16:35). Jesus spent the first thirty years of His life as a child, son, student, brother, and carpenter before the right moment came for Him to begin His ministry (Luke 3:23).

Why doesn't God just bring about His plans in our lives right now? Could it be that one of the ways God makes us like Jesus is through allowing us to express our faith in Him through waiting?

Every once in a while, we get ourselves into a situation that we're not sure how to get out of. Our grades fall dangerously low. Someone at school is making our lives miserable and doesn't seem to want to stop. We drive too fast and get caught—and receive a hefty ticket. We allow our relationship with a parent or sibling to degenerate or become bitter and don't know how to fix things.

The good news is that our God is a God who rescues us. God saves us from sin (Isaiah 57:18), enemies (Deuteronomy 20:4), fear (Psalm 27:2-3), and temptation (1 Corinthians 10:13).

Sometimes we have to face the consequences for our actions as discipline (Hebrews 12:7). But in God's goodness, He promises to be with us in trouble (Psalm 91:15).

Paul's testimony that "the sufferings we have now are nothing compared to the great glory that will be shown to us" (Romans 8:18) is a powerful reminder that God may not be early—but He's always right on time with just what we need.

Is your soul weary with worry? Are you frustrated waiting to know God wants to do in your life? Hold on. God is on the way right now.

Lord my God, I trust in you for protection. Save me and rescue me from those who are chasing me.

Psalm 7:1

REAL LIFE

Escape

AS TOLD TO C. HOPE FLINCHBAUGH

Religious persecution is still a reality for people all over the world. My family was living in Sudan when Muslims declared war on the Christians there. Long before I was born, my dad was a pastor in Sudan, and one night the Muslims attacked our village and torched our church. Families screamed and ran in every direction in the darkness.

Some of the boys were captured and forced to join the Government of Sudan army. Many of the women and girls were captured and sold as slaves to Muslim masters.

My family managed to escape, walking for days before they finally made it to a refugee camp in Kenya. The days turned to years and my father became a pastor to the people around us in the refugee camp. I was born in Kenya and my most vivid memory from the refugee camp is hunger.

The people my dad pastored loved us dearly, and in their desire to obey God, some of them tithed their food provisions. Occasionally, I would see a Christian come to our tent and give my father a handful of cornmeal or a small bag of beans as their tithes to God. More often, the people had no food to tithe. Sometimes my father would give the tithed food to someone poorer than our family.

My mother spent hours in fasting and prayer. Many times we would get food only once a month when the United Nations High Commission for

Refugees dropped off a few items like rice or sugar. I saw my mother feed me and my brothers and sisters for a week from that food. She would only eat one meal and the rest of the month she fasted and prayed that we would all leave Kenya one day. I remember one day when I trapped a bird underneath the round lid of a garbage can. I felt so proud when I came home—my mother cooked a stew for all of us that evening!

During the quiet cool nights in Kenya, I often lay under the stars with the older guys and we talked about what it means to be Sudanese Christians. We made elaborate plans to return to Sudan one day to rescue our Christian families and friends from their Muslim masters—plans that never happened.

God heard my mother's prayers one day and miraculously helped us obtain papers that allowed us to come to America. When I got to the United States, I was amazed by three things: food—piles and piles of food in boxes, bags, cans, and freezers; snow—I'd never seen a snowflake or rolled a snowball until I came here; and freedom—I'm keenly aware of my freedom to pray without the fear of being beaten or kidnapped for exercising my faith.

I've forgiven the Muslims who forced us out of our country and captured or killed many of our family members. One day I want to go back to Africa to help people who are hungry for food and have never heard of Jesus. I want to serve their daily needs, and then tell them the gospel.

ACTION STEP

SET UP A TIME TO SIT DOWN WITH A GRANDPARENT OR PARENT OR OTHER ADULT WHO HAS WALKED WITH GOD A LONG TIME. ASK THEM TO SHARE A FEW STORIES ABOUT WHEN THEY HAD TO WAIT PATIENTLY FOR GOD TO ACT ON A SPECIAL NEED IN HIS OR HER LIFE.

PRAYER

Great is Your faithfulness, O God, my Redeemer. Thank You for being true to Your word by never leaving or forsaking me.

ATTITUDE

THE QUALITY OF OUR LIFE IS MORE DEPENDENT ON OUR PERSPECTIVE THAN OUR CIRCUMSTANCES.

The quickest way to correct the other fellow's attitude is to correct your own.

KING VIDOR

TO THINK ABOUT

- How do you feel when you are around someone who has a consistently negative, critical, cynical attitude? Do you ever notice?
- Are there some negative attitude issues in your life?
- How would you like to improve your attitude? What are some strengths you can build on?

LESSON FOR LIFE

PROMISES

God will...

Renew your mind
Hebrews 8:10

Perfect your character
through patience
James 1:4

Give you patience and
renew your soul
2 Corinthians 4:16

Give you peace and rest
Isaiah 26:3

Hallmarks of a Great Attitude

BIBLE STUDY PASSAGE: PHILIPPIANS 2:3-11

Do not be interested only in your own life, but be interested in the lives of others.

PHILIPPIANS 2:4

Have you had a stinky enough attitude that you didn't even want to be around yourself? A negative, critical, harsh, cynical attitude is poison to relationships—and to your soul.

If you're suffering from a bad case of negativity, here are some sure-fire cures to get your thoughts and perspective moving in the right direction—

- *Smile: "Be full of joy in the Lord always. I will say again, be full of joy" (Philippians 4:4). Our face is often a reflection of what we're feeling inside. Even if you don't feel happy inside, fake it until you feel it.*
- *Say thank you often: "Let the peace that Christ gives control your thinking, because you were all called together in one body to have peace. Always be thankful" (Colossians 3:15). When we take others for granted and see only their faults, our atti-*

216

tude toward them—and theirs toward us—will go downhill
fast. Express appreciation.

In your lives you must
think and act like Christ
Jesus.
Philippians 2:5

- Forgive fast: "Do not let the sun go down on your wrath"
(Ephesians 4:26 NKJV). Unresolved anger and grudges cause
us to hurt others—and ourselves. Even if you have to swallow
your pride and do all the hard work, work things out right now.
Jesus says don't even go to church without clearing things up
with your brother (Matthew 5:23-25).
- Be proactive: "Let us think about each other and help each other
to show love and do good deeds" (Hebrews 10:24). Instead of
moaning and groaning and complaining about how bad things
are, act. Inaction is a breeding ground for negativity.
- Watch your words: "When you talk, do not say harmful things,
but say what people need" (Ephesians 4:29). What we say has
a tremendous impact on how we feel. Do your words make
you more or less positive?
- Cheer up someone else: "By helping each other with your troubles, you truly obey the law of Christ" (Galatians 6:2). If you're
feeling sorry for yourself, find someone who really has problems, and help them see life through the eyes of faith and hope
again. It will help you, too.

Rejoice. Your new attitude begins today!

 REAL LIFE

My Brother

I had never really talked about it, so it guess it was true he couldn't have known, but I was still furious at my older brother. He was seventeen and I was fifteen. We fought some, but also had a lot of fun together. But now he had just asked a girl that I had my eye on to the school dance—and she said yes. So with no driver's license, I was stuck at home and he was set to go out with the girl of my dreams. If that wasn't bad enough, he brought her and another couple over to the house for pictures before their big romantic dinner plans.

Unfortunately, I was out front with my skateboard. I looked like a total idiot. And I was steamed.

That event happened six months ago. And I have to confess, for the next five months it was brutal at my house. I didn't talk to anyone for about a week. My mom kept asking what was wrong, which drove me crazy and made me even madder. This made my dad mad, and he got in my face. We had an unbelievable shouting match. I know our neighbors from a couple houses away could hear us. He grounded me for two weeks and I let him know I didn't care—I didn't want to go anywhere or see anyone anyway.

My brother, who I thought started the whole mess, got in my face next. "What's your problem?" he demanded.

I told him to mind his own business and gave him a push—he may be older, but he's not bigger. We ended up throwing punches and now both of us were grounded.

I didn't get in any more fist fights, but I was basically like this with everyone. My parents were shocked. My brother was furious. My friends at church and school barely recognized me. I didn't care. I was mad. I was resentful. I didn't like anybody.

I skipped school one day and got an in-school suspension. When my soccer coach called me to his office to let me know he was considering kicking me off the team before the season even started, I finally woke up. Sports have always been a big deal to me and my family—my brother is on the football team. I had a chance to get playing time on varsity as a sophomore. I realized my attitude—not others' actions—was about to mess everything up for me.

It's been a month since then. Things aren't 100% right between me and my family. The hardest step was admitting to myself my attitude stunk. Next hardest was apologizing.

But God's helping me control my anger.

I finally told my brother what made me mad in the first place. We've both agreed we won't let a girl come between us again. Unless I ask her out first!

ACTION STEP

ATTITUDE IS SO FOUNDATIONAL TO THE QUALITY OF LIFE WE LIVE THAT MAYBE WE NEED TO GET BACK TO BASICS. BEFORE YOU LAUGH THIS ACTIVITY OFF AS TOO SIMPLE, ASK YOURSELF: HOW BAD DO I NEED A BETTER ATTITUDE?

GO TO A CRAFT STORE OR THE SCHOOL SUPPLIES SECTION OF ANOTHER RETAIL OUTLET. BUY NOTECARDS AND STICKERS—ESPECIALLY GOLD STARS. LABEL A NOTECARD FOR EVERY DAY OF THIS COMING WEEK. EVERY TIME YOU EXPRESS A POSITIVE ATTITUDE, ADD A BRIGHT, COLORFUL, HAPPY STICKER TO THE CARD. WHEN YOU EXPRESS A NEGATIVE ATTITUDE, ADHERE A FROWNING FACE OR OTHER SAD STICKER.

AT THE END OF THE WEEK, TAKE A LOOK AND SEE HOW YOU'RE DOING.

PRAYER

Father, You have given me a great life. Help me enjoy the wonderful things You've given me by having a great attitude.

CHURCH

WE ALL NEED A GROUP OF FRIENDS WHO WILL HELP US GROW SPIRITUALLY.

The Bible knows nothing of solitary religion.

JOHN WESLEY

 ## TO THINK ABOUT

- Do you feel like you have a group of friends who accept you as you are—and help you grow spiritually?
- Have you ever tried to be someone else or done things you don't agree with just so you could fit in?
- Are you accepting of others?   Do you help them feel like they belong?   Do you help people grow closer to God?

LESSON FOR LIFE

PROMISES

God will...

Minister to you through
others
1 Thessalonians 3:12
1Peter 4:10

Give you joy through
others
John 17:13

Teach you through
others
Colossians 3:16

Make you strong through
others
2 Thessalonians 2:17

Come Together

BIBLE STUDY PASSAGE: ACTS 4:23-35

You should not stay away from the church meetings, as some are doing, but you should meet together and encourage each other. Do this even more as you see the day coming.

HEBREWS 10:25

We all need a group of friends who like us and accept us for who we are.

One great place for that to happen is through an active youth group in a great church.

There are some things we can only get from meeting with other Christians—

> • *Mutual encouragement: "You should not stay away from the church meetings, as some are doing, but you should meet together and encourage each other" (Hebrews 10:25). It is dangerous to think that we don't need the encouragement and support of others who love God. And even if our relationship with God is fine without church attendance, shouldn't we be there to*

222

encourage others?

- *Accountability: "Fools think they are doing right, but the wise listen to advice" (Proverbs 12:15). Without accountability, we can get ourselves in trouble, and sharing our lives with a circle of church friends can keep us far from sin.*

- *The teaching of God's Word: "They spent their time learning the apostles' teaching, sharing, breaking bread, and praying together" (Acts 2:42). Yes, it's very possible—and important—to grow in knowledge of the Bible from individual study and reflection, but as the writer of Proverbs tells us: "As iron sharpens iron, so people can improve each other" (27:17). We need to interact on what God's Word really means with others.*

- *Friendship: "This is my prayer for you: that your love will grow more and more; that you will have knowledge and understanding with your love" (Philippians 1:9). It is true that we are influenced by those we spend significant time with. If all your significant relationships are with people who don't support the lifestyle God wants for you, you are putting yourself at risk. Find people who fan your desire to know God better, and spend time with them.*

The truth is that we all need each other—we need a community to belong with. The good news is that church is a great place to interact with people who encourage us.

Glorify the Lord with me, and let us praise his name together.
Psalm 34:3

REAL LIFE

P.K.

JACOB P. AS TOLD TO T. SUZANNE ELLER

I've been a P.K. (pastor's kid) from the time I was born.   When I went to school, I hesitated when people asked me what my dad did.   And when kids mocked my family, God, and me, I almost became ashamed of what my dad did.   I wanted people to accept me for who I was.

I decided to leave school and do home school for a while.   After a couple of years, I returned to public school, vowing that this time things would be different.   I dressed in baggy clothes and bleached my hair.   I started hanging out with people who lived very differently from my beliefs, but made me feel accepted.

Music opened the door to more social opportunities for me—I was a natural on the drums, and when I joined the school jazz band, people were impressed with my ability.   Then I received an offer to play in a punk band— the Burnouts.   I wasn't thrilled with the whole punk scene, but I stayed in it because playing in a band brought attention and popularity.

We Burnouts became pretty well known at school, and soon started playing parties.   The parties we played could get pretty wild—the police even shut down a few.

At this point, I was rebelling against God, and I knew it.   God was waiting for me to recommit my life to Him, but I wanted to keep the acceptance from my peers that I had worked so hard to earn.

Then my parents took us to visit my cousin, and I attended church with their family one night. When I walked into the youth group, I was surprised by how freely everyone worshiped God—no one seemed to care what people thought of them. It hit me that God was in that room. Away from everything and everybody back home, I could see clearly that God loved me—not as a P.K., but for who I was.

That night I opened my heart and gave my struggle with rejection and acceptance to God. In that moment, I knew I needed to start going back to my church youth group.

When I returned home, I quit the band. I called our guitar player and told him that if I was going to play, it had to be for God. When I lost my position in the band, I lost my girlfriend. The losses continued as friends walked away, people who only liked me because I was a Burnout.

I started telling people at school about God. I shared my story with a friend who later got so hooked on the Word of God that he knows it better than I do. I met a girl who loves God—and likes me for me.

I still play the drums, but now it's for my church worship team. I've been writing music that God gives me, and one day I plan to lead worship.

Now I don't fear what people say when they ask me what my dad does. It doesn't matter what they think. I look them straight in the eye and tell them my dad is a pastor.

In fact, I plan to be just like him in a few years.

ACTION STEP

YOU MAY BE A GREAT CHURCH ATTENDEE, OR YOU MAY BE STRUGGLING TO GET THROUGH THE CHURCH DOORS ON A CONSISTENT BASIS. WHEREVER YOU ARE, DO SOMETHING THIS WEEK TO STEP UP YOUR GAME. FIND AN ACCOUNT-ABILITY GROUP AT YOUR CHURCH—OR FORM ONE WITH THREE OR FOUR OTHER STUDENTS. MAKE A COMMITMENT TO YOURSELF TO ATTEND SERVICE EVERY WEEK FOR TWO MONTHS, AND REWARD YOURSELF FOR MAKING GOOD ON YOUR GOAL. MAYBE RIGHT NOW YOU'RE NEEDING TO FIND A CHURCH—MAKE A PLAN TO VISIT A FEW CHURCHES OVER THE NEXT FEW SUNDAYS AND ASK GOD TO SHOW YOU WHERE TO PLUG IN.

TAKE COMFORT IN THE THOUGHT THAT YOUR LIFE WILL BECOME RICHER AS YOU SEEK GOD ALONGSIDE OTHERS.

PRAYER

Father God, thank You for giving us friends to help us along. Guide me today as I look for ways to connect more deeply with others.

DEPENDENCE V. INDEPENDENCE

GOD IS LEADING YOU TO NEW LEVELS OF MATURITY SO YOU CAN ACHIEVE HEALTHY INDEPENDENCE—WITHOUT LOSING YOUR RESPECT FOR AND CLOSE BONDS WITH YOUR PARENTS.

The truly strong person is not the one who never needs help, but the one who can ask for it when he does.

ANONYMOUS

 TO THINK ABOUT

- Are you happy with where you are in life—or are you impatient to grow up right now?
- Do you have a healthy relationship with your parents and other adults in your life?
- How ready are you to be out on your own?

LESSON FOR LIFE

Mature and Complete

*Let your patience show itself perfectly in what you do.
Then you will be perfect and complete and will have
everything you need.*

JAMES 1:4

*I can't wait until I get my driver's license. I want a job so I can
have my own money. I'm counting the days until I can leave home
and head to college. My parents treat me like a kid!*

It's great to grow up—but don't be in too big of a hurry. Being
independent has its own set of pressures. Of course, some of us are
a little reluctant to be out on our own—and need a little push. But
most of us welcome new levels of independence. Just remember—

• *Independence requires more work than dependence: "If you want
to build a tower, you first sit down and decide how much it will
cost, to see if you have enough money to finish the job" (Luke
14:28). When we think of being independent, we usually focus on
the benefits, not the costs. Don't take for granted all that your
parents provide and do for you or you may be in for a rude awak-
ening. There are guys who are shocked to discover that laundry*

doesn't get cleaned and folded by itself.

- *Independence requires more maturity than dependence:* "We must become like a mature person, growing until we become like Christ and have his perfection.   Then we will no longer be babies." (Ephesians 4:13-14). If you didn't have an adult presence in your life to make sure you were on track, how well would you do in church attendance? Eating your vegetables? Keeping your living space clean? Staying on top of homework?

- *Independence is never completely separate from dependence:* "Obey your parents as the Lord wants," (Ephesians 6:1). It's true, your parents want you to be more independent. Of course, they want you to do it in the right way and over time. But don't forget, you will always need your parents. They will always be a source of insight and comfort. Don't forget that even the strongest, smartest, most responsible individual needs help from time to time.

- *Independence can create conflict:* "So a man will leave his father and mother and be united with his wife, and the two will become one body" (Genesis 2:24). As you transition from kid to adult, you won't handle all situations well—and neither will parents. Be respectful always. Listen hard always. Be ready to ask for forgiveness and to forgive. Sometimes you will have to judge your parents' hearts and not their words—just as they will with you.

Though the Lord is supreme, he takes care of those who are humble, but he stays away from the proud.
Psalm 138:6

229

Shouldering the Load

JESSICA INMAN

Sitting in my car, I hurled curses at my shoulder joint. I had just arrived at work, and my unluckily loose shoulder had dislocated when I so foolishly moved my arm from the passenger seat to my seat belt.

I scrambled for my phone. After calling my boss to let him know why I wasn't immediately heading into the warehouse, I called my mom, almost without thinking. I asked if she could please start heading my direction, in case I couldn't put my shoulder back in. She said she would.

Time to wait. Between attempts to prod my arm back into place, I allowed myself to think about the calls I'd just made. Part of me wished I hadn't had to call my mom—I wished I didn't have to depend on her to come get me.

Another part of me, though, really wanted her to get here. Now.

When she arrived, my arm was still dangling sickly at my side, and I eased into the passenger seat of her car. As she steered delicately out of the parking lot, I gave in to the urge to cry.

I think it scared her. She said, "It'll be okay. They'll put it back in." She kept saying things like that, too, throughout an evening of waiting rooms and X-rays. We returned home and ate takeout chicken, and she scolded me for getting my own ice out of the freezer.

The next day, my mom had the day off and offered to buy me lunch before we went to pick up my car from the warehouse parking lot. We walked into the semi-authentic Chinese place in our small suburb and sat down. As Mom visited the restroom, I gazed at the fake grain of the plastic picnic-style table-cloth and Solo cups of neon orange sweet-and-sour sauce.

My mom was always buying me hope chest items like dishes and knick-knacks, always wanting to talk about absolutely everything. And I was always trying to prove how much I could do things on my own and didn't need her help with anything. Today, though, with my arm in a sling, I couldn't do things on my own, and I did need help.

Later that evening, I asked meekly if she could put my hair in a ponytail—my arm was still stiff and disinclined to move toward the back of my head.

It was a good ponytail—better than the ones I do for myself. I told her that. She smiled and said, "I've done a lot of them."

I can't wait for the day I buy my mom a set of dishes or table linens or an addition to her crystal bird collection as a symbol that I'm officially inde-pendent—but also as an expression of gratitude. She'll always be my mom, and I'll always be grateful for her help.

ACTION STEP

YOU MIGHT BE SEVERAL YEARS AWAY FROM REAL INDEPENDENCE. YOU MIGHT BE ONLY A YEAR OR TWO FROM MOVING OUT. ONE IMPORTANT AREA OF LIFE THAT IS AN INDICATOR OF OUR MATURITY IS MONEY. DO YOU HAVE A CHECKBOOK YET? DO YOU KNOW HOW TO KEEP AND BALANCE ONE? TALK TO YOUR PARENTS ABOUT SETTING UP AN ACCOUNT (THEY WILL HAVE TO CO-SIGN WITH YOU). ASK THEM AND YOUR BANKER TO TEACH YOU HOW TO KEEP TRACK OF WHAT YOU'VE SPENT AND EARNED—AND MAKE SURE WHAT YOU'VE EARNED IS MORE THAN WHAT YOU'VE SPENT!

PRAYER

Father God, help me stretch my wings and conquer new challenges today— without forgetting that You help me along when I need it.

ALCOHOL

ALCOHOL USE MAY BE COMMON AMONG TEENS, BUT IT HAS MANY NEGATIVE CONSEQUENCES FOR YOUR BODY AND SOUL.

*One reason I don't drink is that I want
to know when I am having a good time.*

LADY ASTOR

 To Think About

- How common is drug and alcohol abuse in your school?
- Have you been presented with opportunities to drink?
- What are some of the negative consequences of drinking and drug use that you've seen?

LESSON FOR LIFE

PROMISES

God will...

Bless your obedience
Psalm 119:2

Provide everything for
you to enjoy life
1 Timothy 6:17

Take care of you as you
make Him your first
priority
Matthew 6:33

Drugs and Alcohol

BIBLE STUDY PASSAGE: EPHESIANS 5:1-20

*Do not be drunk with wine, which will ruin you, but be
filled with the Spirit.*

EPHESIANS 5:18

The media commonly portrays the use of alcohol and even
illegal drugs by teens as fun and harmless. A number of school
and community programs like DARE (Drug Abuse Resistance
Education), MADD (Mothers Against Drunk Driving), and SADD
(Students Against Drunk Driving) work hard to counteract these
incomplete and misleading images.

But face it, as a teenager, you will be faced with many
opportunities to drink or try illegal drugs—and in many cases,
the opportunity will seem very appealing.

How will you decide what to say? A couple of reminders
might help—

* *Alcohol is against the law for teenagers*—*"So you must yield to
the government, not only because you might be punished, but
because you know it is right" (Romans 13:5). Once you deter-*

mine that the law doesn't really matter or apply to you, you are saying that authority isn't important for your life. You can protest issues of injustice, but you don't honor God or protect your soul by simply ignoring the law.

• Alcohol impairs judgment and lowers inhibitions—"Wine and beer make people loud and uncontrolled; it is not wise to get drunk on them" (Proverbs 20:1). Alcohol alters your ability to think and see clearly. You will be less picky about what you do, and may even risk your purity. One of the sad realities of drinking at any age is that it becomes an opportunity for some predators to take advantage of members of the opposite sex.

• Alcohol is dangerous—"Do not be drunk with wine, which will ruin you, but be filled with the Spirit" (Ephesians 5:18). Alcohol contributes to more than half of all road accidents that involve teenagers. Alcohol makes many teens become more aggressive and get into fights and become verbally abusive—they often think they are just being funny.

• Alcohol can lead to future problems. The younger a person is when they start drinking, the more likely they will have a drinking problem as an adult. Anyone who has lived in a home with an alcoholic parent knows what a drain on finances and all other forms of emotional stability it causes.

How terrible it will be for people who rise early in the morning to look for strong drink, who stay awake late at night, becoming drunk with wine.
Isaiah 5:11

235

REAL LIFE

The Party's Over

I know it wasn't my fault, but I still feel guilty for my part in what happened. Jamie and I had been best friends since kindergarten. We did everything together—cheer squad, volleyball team, summers where we almost lived at the swimming pool. We also attended church together, which made our bond even stronger.

But then when we moved over to the high school, things changed. She started hanging out with some kids I wasn't comfortable with. She went to some parties with lots of alcohol and more, and I just wouldn't go.

One weekend, she told her mother she was spending the weekend at a friend's house—my house. She really wanted to go to a party and was using me to cover for her. I never said anything to her mom.

The party kicked off Friday night, continued Saturday morning, and picked up steam again on Saturday night. This kid's parents were gone for the weekend.

Twenty-four hours after it started, about thirty of the partygoers became ill, some vomiting blood, others convulsing, still others experiencing blurred vision and breathing difficulties.

Jamie died. My best friend for years was gone forever.

The autopsy and blood tests revealed that she had ingested high levels of methanol. The party host had purchased "moonshine" from a nineteen-year-old acquaintance. The moonshine was a mixture of an industrial solvent and punch. It was cheap and gave a huge buzz. Some of the kids had downed as many as three glasses of the brew.

When Jamie's mother was called to the house on Sunday night, they were attempting to resuscitate her, to no avail. The party was over and so was Jamie's life.

I promised myself then and there that I would never join the party crowd. Life's too precious. After not being able to look Jamie's mom in the eyes at the funeral, I also promised I'd never cover for a friend again. Like I said, life's too precious.

ACTION STEP

IS THE TEMPTATION TO DRINK AN ISSUE FOR YOU? WHAT MAKES IT SO TEMPTING? DO YOU WANT TO DRINK TO NUMB PAIN IN YOUR LIFE, OR TO FIT IN WITH A CERTAIN GROUP OF PEOPLE?

YOUR BEST SHOT AT KEEPING A COMMITMENT NOT TO DRINK IS TO SURROUND YOURSELF WITH PEOPLE WHO WILL SUPPORT THAT DECISION. TAKE A STEP THIS WEEK TO REINFORCE A RELATIONSHIP WITH A YOUTH GROUP FRIEND, AND LOOK FOR AN OPPORTUNITY TO DISCUSS YOUR COMMITMENT TO PURITY IN EACH OF YOUR LIVES.

PRAYER

Father, I really do want to honor You with my decisions. Please help me rid my life of things that don't reflect respect for You.

GOD IS OUR FATHER

GOD LOVES US AND WATCHES OVER US AS ONLY A GOOD AND LOVING FATHER CAN DO.

*When we call on God, he bends down His ear to listen,
as a father bends down to listen to his little child.*

ELIZABETH CHARLES

 TO THINK ABOUT

- What are different characteristics of a great father?
- What are different things you appreciate about your father?
- What are different ways that God wants to be a Father to us?

LESSON FOR LIFE

PROMISES

God will...

Help you
Psalm 10:14

Take away fear
Romans 8:15

Speak to you
Isaiah 48:17

Take up the cause of the
fatherless
Malachi 3:5

Who Is Your Daddy?

BIBLE STUDY PASSAGE: PSALM 139

But to all who did accept him and believe in him he gave the right to become children of God.   They did not become his children in any human way—by any human parents or human desire.   They were born of God

JOHN 1:12-13

Our lives are so much richer and fuller because God is our Father. Consider just a few of the blessings that come from knowing God is our Father—

- *We are protected: "Those who go to God Most High for safety will be protected by the Almighty" (Psalm 91:1). Even if some bad things have happened in your life, God will never allow anything to happen that would separate you from Him in all eternity.*
- *We have our needs met: "My God will use his wonderful riches in Christ Jesus to give you everything you need" (Philippians 4:19). The God who created the universe and who owns everything in it promises to provide for us exactly what we need to survive and thrive. Even if you are from a family that struggles*

240

financially, you will have everything you need for a bright today and tomorrow.

- We have Someone who loves us: "For you did not receive the spirit of bondage again to fear, but you received the Spirit of adoption by whom we cry out, 'Abba, Father'" (Romans 8:15 NKJV). God loves us so much that He wants us to call Him "Daddy." That is not what you call someone who is preoccupied and uncaring. It is what you call the One who adores you.
- We are never alone: "If I rise with the sun in the east and settle in the west beyond the sea, even there you would guide me. With your right hand you would hold me" (Psalm 139:9-10). Just like an earthly father who tucked us in at night when we were little kids, our Heavenly Father never makes us walk alone in the dark. Sure, life is tough at times, but with the most powerful Daddy in the world, we don't have to be afraid. One of the sweetest promises in the Bible is that God adopts orphans in a special way. So even if we don't have a father, we still have a Daddy.
- We have a wise guide: "You keep your loving promise and lead the people you have saved" (Exodus 15:13). Fathers are put on this earth to raise kids, to give them wisdom and counsel. Isn't it good to know that you have a Heavenly Father who is all wise and knowing? When you turn to Him for advice and direction, you can't go wrong!

God is in his holy Temple. He is a father to orphans, and he defends the widows.

Psalm 68:5

241

REAL LIFE

The Father I'd Always Wanted

KATIE MINTER JONES

Father's Day had always been difficult for me. But this year was especially hard because my father had recently died, along with him the hope of ever hearing him say, "I love you" or having him show me that he cared about me.

The Saturday before Father's Day, I had a long list of errands to run. I tried not to think about the upcoming holiday, but as I drove, my mind was flooded with memories of life without him and thoughts of how my life could have been, if he had only cared.

He'd left when I was an infant, my mother young and unable to cope as a single parent. I grew up shuffled between different relatives, foster homes, and a children's home.

When I was little, whenever I was scared or sad, I'd dream that he would come rescue me and I would be a "daddy's girl." Sadly, my dreams would never come true. He'd never tuck me in, kiss me goodnight, bandage my skinned knees, hold me in his lap, or tell me that he loved me.

I thought about how I felt when he contacted me as a teenager. I was so excited—maybe my dreams would come true—but I was quickly disappointed. The first time we met, he told me not to call him Daddy because he was an elected official and the people in his district didn't know about me.

My eyes filled with tears as I remembered scanning the audience at my graduation, hoping to catch a glimpse of him, but he hadn't come. When I married, I walked down the aisle alone because he wasn't there to give me away. I'd hoped that he would become a part of my children's lives, but he never came to see my children when they were born. They never knew the joy of having a grandfather.

For many years, I was angry and bitter toward him. Then, I realized that in order for me to have peace, I had to forgive him. But there was still a void—a deep feeling of emptiness and loss. I had prayed thousands of times asking God to heal the pain and fill the emptiness, but that prayer always seemed to be unanswered.

Driving down the road, I again prayed my "unanswered" prayer.

In my state of wistful prayer, I had missed my turn, so I turned on the next side street.

As I looked for a place to turn around, I saw a church sign that I wouldn't have seen if I hadn't missed my turn. Suddenly, overwhelmed with His comfort, I thanked my Father for always being there for me and loving me.

The sign's timely message read, "I am the Father that you always wanted." My Father had answered my prayer when I needed it the most.

ACTION STEP

FOR A FUN CHANGE OF PACE, TRY AN ARTISTIC ACTIVITY. FIRST, ASK YOUR MOM OR DAD IF YOU CAN SEE A COPY OF YOUR BIRTH CERTIFICATE. THEN CREATE A SPIRITUAL BIRTH CERTIFICATE BASED ON WHEN YOU TRULY KNEW THAT GOD WAS YOUR FATHER.

PRAYER

Lord God, I'm amazed that You would take it on yourself to be my Father. Thank You for searching for me and taking care of me. I love You.

A PRAYER FOR YOUR SOUL

The most important soul matter, of course, is having a relationship with God. Everything in our lives—everything in our entire existence—has new, eternal meaning when we understand that God loves us and has made a way to save us through Jesus Christ. All of this may be new to you. If you'd like to know that you have a lasting relationship with God through Jesus, pray this prayer:

Heavenly Father, I come to You admitting that I am a sinner. I believe that Your Son, Jesus, died on the cross and rose from the dead to take away my sins. Jesus, I choose to follow You and ask that You fill me with the Holy Spirit so that I can understand more about You. Thank You for adopting me, and thank You that I am now a child of God. Amen.

How to Read and Study the Bible

One of the most important keys to nurturing your soul is consistent reading and studying of Scripture. If you're a new Bible reader, be patient with yourself! Learn to study and apply God's Word one step at a time.

1. **Have your own Bible.** *Your own Bible is the one that has your name in it, the one that you not only carry to church, but even remember to bring home with you. You need a Bible that you cherish and keep close at hand.*

2. **Begin with prayer.** *Every time you sit down to read your Bible, ask God to speak to you through Scripture. Let Him know you are ready and willing to hear His voice.*

3. **Plan a Bible-reading schedule.** *You will profit more from Bible reading if you study entire books at a time, not just parts here and there. So map out a good Bible-reading schedule, planning which books to work through several at a time.*

4. **Use a study method.** *Discipline in Bible study is just like discipline in any other area—discipline leads to positive and healthy experiences in our lives.*

If you keep a notebook or prayer journal, you might start a section titled "My Time in the Word." As you learn one simple Bible study method, you'll see how a notebook can be used to make your time in the Word more effective.

Step One:

LOOK FOR THE BIG PICTURE

Before focusing on several verses of a particular chapter, get an overall idea of the book you are reading. Try to find out who is writing the book, to whom, and why. Many Bibles contain a short introduction to each book of the Bible with a lot of this information given. Another way to do this is to read the entire book quickly; if it is a longer book, simply skim through it and note the paragraph headings printed in your Bible. You're not trying to read every word, just get acquainted with the flow and feeling of the book.

Step Two:

SELECT A STUDY PASSAGE

Once you have an idea of the big picture, you'll want to study the entire book in chunks—anywhere from a few verses to an entire chapter at a time.

When you study a passage, what counts is quality of reading, not quantity. One caution: You will not want to break up paragraphs, or you will lose the writer's train of thought.

Step Three:

READ THE STUDY PASSAGE SEVERAL TIMES

After you choose the verses you are going to study, read that section of scripture at least two times. Three or four times would be better. And remember, you set the pace—you can choose to study a chapter or just a few verses. What counts is that you grow in an understanding of God's Word.

Step Four:

SEARCH FOR MAJOR TRUTHS

As you read through your study passage for the third or fourth time, note the key thoughts found there. What does the writer want the people who read this to understand? Look for commands to be obeyed, warnings to be heeded, promises to be claimed, and truths to be believed.

Set aside a space in your journal for you to jot down these key thoughts and major truths.

Step Five:

ASK QUESTIONS

Now is the time to raise questions that come to your mind. Not everything in Scripture is immediately or easily understood. Do not be surprised or intimidated by this fact.

Write down your questions in your notebook or journal. Here are several places where you can go to get answers to these questions.

• **Scripture:** Use a concordance or study Bible to look up passages of scripture that deal with the subject you're studying—often, one scripture can help explain another.

• **Commentaries:** Commentaries study and explain Bible passages a little at a time. Your church library probably contains several sets of commentaries you could borrow.

• **Pastors and teachers:** Your pastor and Sunday school teachers may not be able to give you an answer right away, but they will be willing to search for answers with you.

Step Six:

PUTTING IT INTO PRACTICE

You need to apply the Bible to your life now. "Do not merely listen to the word ... Do what it says" (1:22) was James' advice.

Is there something you are doing that you shouldn't be doing? Is there something you are not doing that you need to be doing? Is there something about God or Jesus or the Holy Spirit that you did not know before? Do you need to be more sensitive to someone at work? Do you need to seek someone's forgiveness? Do you need to forgive someone?

Step Seven:

NOTE A VERSE TO REMEMBER

The final step in your Bible study is to take one last look at your study passage and write down a verse or two that you want to remember most. Memorizing scripture is a terrific discipline. It allows you to take scripture with you, even when you don't or can't have your Bible at hand.

Writing out a key verse will make remembering it much easier for you. It is a good start to memorizing it also.

May God cause your soul to stretch and grow
as you embark on a journey through His Word!

Acknowledgements

"The Best Summer Job Ever" © Mark Gilroy Communications. Used by permission. All rights reserved.

"Maximum Security" © Neely Arrington. Used by permission. All rights reserved.

"Billy the Bully" © Robin Bayne. Used by permission. All rights reserved.

"Steady as a PB&J" © Sandra Railsback. Used by permission. All rights reserved.

"The Day the Sea Parted Me" © Lana Comstock. Used by permission. All rights reserved.

"The Father I'd Always Wanted" © Katie Minter Jones. Used by permission. All rights reserved.

"The Party's Over" © Mark Gilroy Communications. Used by permission. All rights reserved.

"Shouldering the Load" © Jessica Inman. Used by permission. All rights reserved.

"P.K." © Eller, T. Suzanne. From Real Teens, Real Stories Real Life, published 2002.
    Used by permission of Cook Communications Ministries.

"My Brother" © Mark Gilroy Communications. Used by permission. All rights reserved.

"Escape" © C. Hope Flinchbaugh. Used by permission. All rights reserved.

"Just What I Needed" © Jessica Inman. Used by permission. All rights reserved.

"Why Me?" © Candace Marra. Used by permission. All rights reserved.

"Peace of Mind" © Mark Gilroy Communications. Used by permission. All rights reserved.

"Terrified on Timpanogos Mountain" © Patricia Lorenz. Used by permission. All rights reserved.

"Congratulations, Becky" © Jessica Inman. Used by permission. All rights reserved.

"Per 'Er There, Pal" © Mark Gilroy. Used by permission. All rights reserved.

"Circle of Friends" © Eller, T. Suzanne. From Real Teens, Real Stories Real Life, published 2002.
    Used by permission of Cook Communications Ministries.

"Tough Love" © Stephen A. Peterson. Used by permission. All rights reserved.

"In the Right Place at the Right Time" © C. Hope Flinchbaugh. Used by permission. All rights reserved.

255

Your Story

Has there been a time in your life when you encountered God in a powerful way that changed and enriched your soul? Would your story encourage others to grow closer to God and improve their lives?

WE WOULD LOVE TO CONSIDER YOUR STORY FOR FUTURE EDITIONS OF SOUL MATTERS. PLEASE SHARE YOUR STORY TODAY, WON'T YOU? FOR WRITER'S GUIDELINES, UPCOMING TITLES, AND SUBMISSION PROCEDURES, VISIT:

www.soulmattersbooks.com

Or send a postage-paid, self-addressed envelope to:

**Mark Gilroy Communications, Inc.
6528 E. 101st Street, Suite 416
Tulsa, Oklahoma 74133-6754**